D0616108

降击神通

AVATAR

THE LAST AIRBENDER™

Created by
Bryan Konietzko
Michael Dante DiMartino

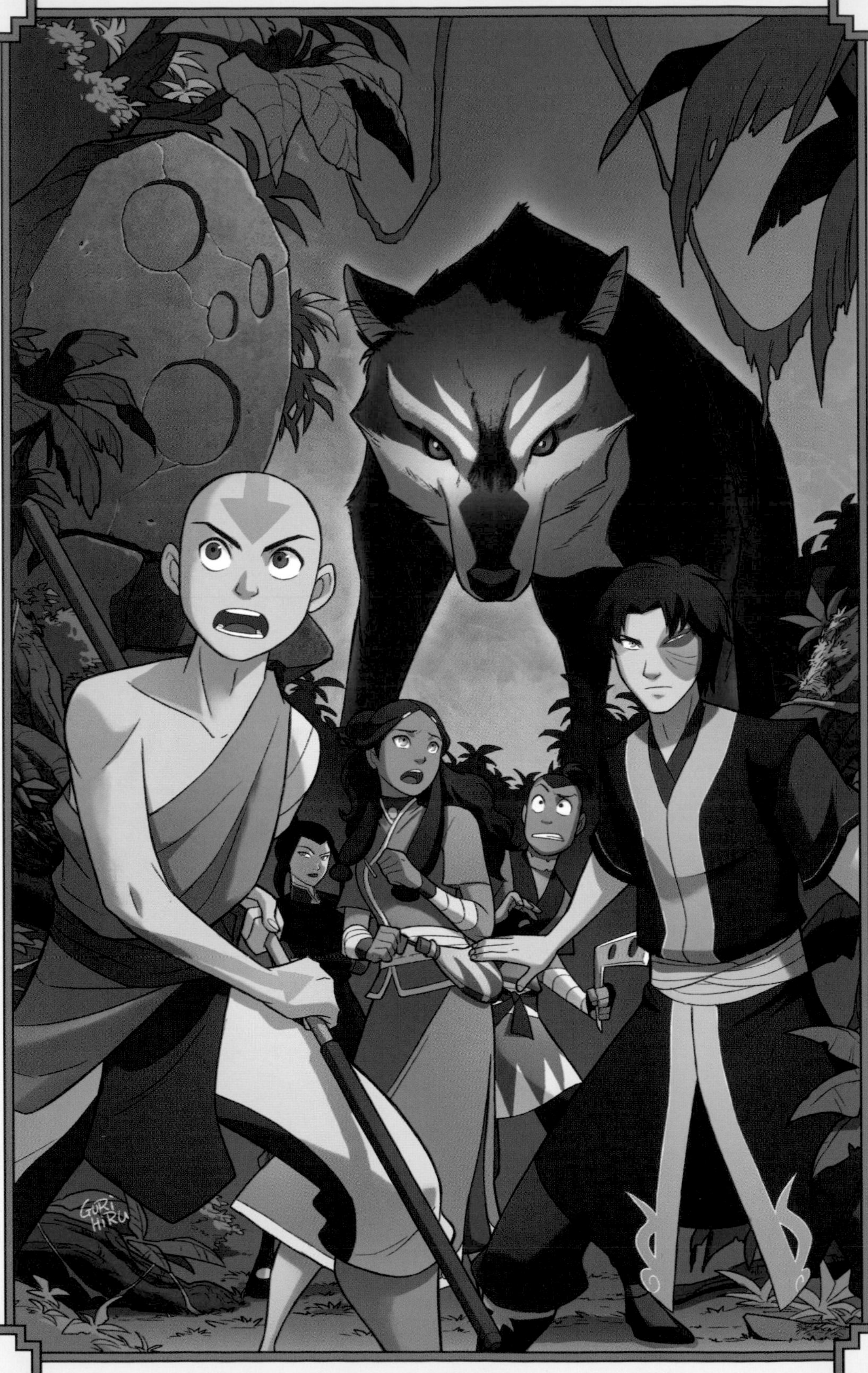
GURI HIRU

nickelodeon™

降击神通

AVATAR

THE LAST AIRBENDER™

THE SEARCH · PART TWO

script
GENE LUEN YANG

art and cover
GURIHIRU

lettering
MICHAEL HEISLER

DARK HORSE BOOKS

publisher
MIKE RICHARDSON

collection designer
JUSTIN COUCH

assistant editor
IAN TUCKER

editor
DAVE MARSHALL

Nickelodeon Avatar: The Last Airbender™—The Search Part 2

© 2013 Viacom International, Inc. All rights reserved. Nickelodeon, Nickelodeon Avatar: The Last Airbender, and all related titles, logos, and characters are trademarks of Viacom International, Inc. All other material, unless otherwise specified, is © 2013 Dark Horse Comics LLC. Dark Horse Books® and the Dark Horse logo are registered trademarks of Dark Horse Comics LLC. All rights reserved. No portion of this publication may be reproduced or transmitted, in any form or by any means, without the express written permission of Dark Horse Comics LLC. Names, characters, places, and incidents featured in this publication either are the product of the author's imagination or are used fictitiously. Any resemblance to actual persons (living or dead), events, institutions, or locales, without satiric intent, is coincidental.

Special thanks to Linda Lee, Kat van Dam, James Salerno, and Joan Hilty at Nickelodeon, and to Bryan Konietzko and Michael Dante DiMartino.

Published by
Dark Horse Books
A division of
Dark Horse Comics LLC
10956 SE Main Street
Milwaukie, OR 97222

DarkHorse.com
Nick.com

To find a comics shop in your area, visit comicshoplocator.com

First edition: July 2013
ISBN 978-1-61655-190-2

9 10

Printed in China

AZULA...

≡GASP!≡ H-HOW DID *YOU* GET THE JUMP ON *ME?!*

GIVE UP THIS FUTILE QUEST, MY DAUGHTER. GO HOME. THE THRONE IS ZUKO'S DESTINY. YOURS LIES ELSEWHERE.

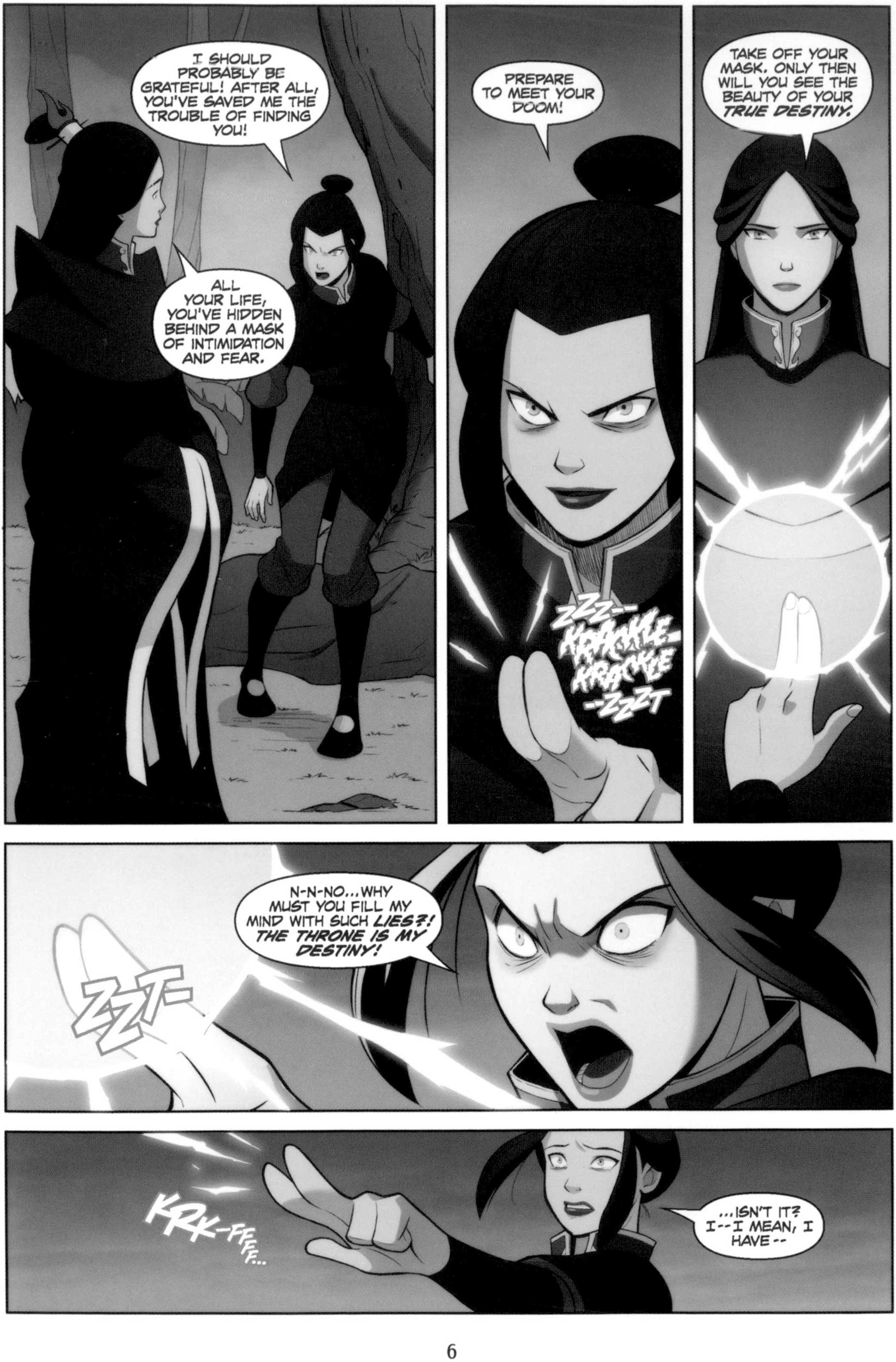
I SHOULD PROBABLY BE GRATEFUL! AFTER ALL, YOU'VE SAVED ME THE TROUBLE OF FINDING YOU!
ALL YOUR LIFE, YOU'VE HIDDEN BEHIND A MASK OF INTIMIDATION AND FEAR.
PREPARE TO MEET YOUR DOOM!
ZZZ--KRACKLE-KRACKLE--ZZZT
TAKE OFF YOUR MASK. ONLY THEN WILL YOU SEE THE BEAUTY OF YOUR TRUE DESTINY.
ZZT-
N-N-NO...WHY MUST YOU FILL MY MIND WITH SUCH LIES?! THE THRONE IS MY DESTINY!
KRK-FFFF...
...ISN'T IT? I--I MEAN, I HAVE--

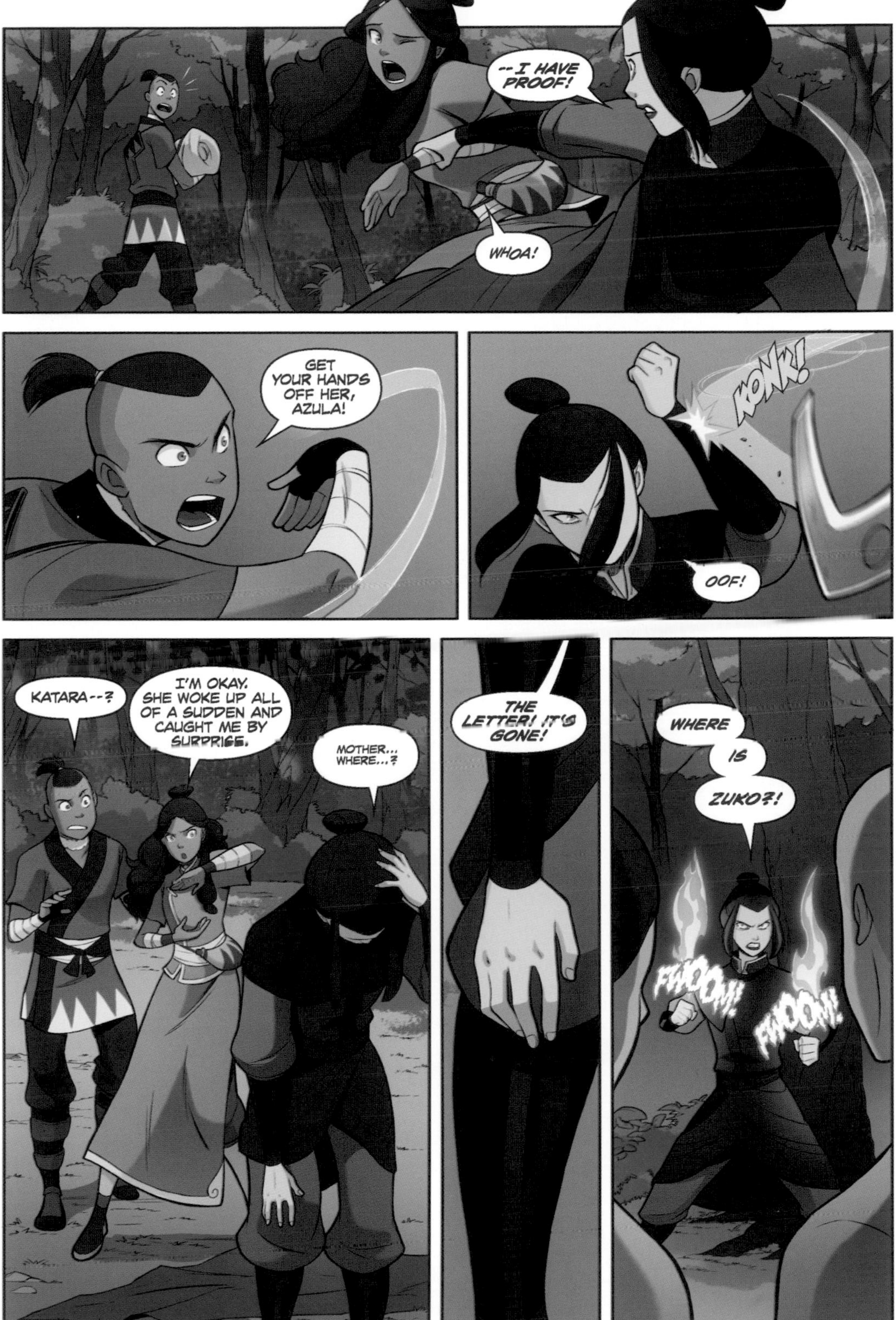
--I HAVE PROOF!
WHOA!
GET YOUR HANDS OFF HER, AZULA!
KONK!
OOF!
KATARA--?
I'M OKAY. SHE WOKE UP ALL OF A SUDDEN AND CAUGHT ME BY SURPRISE.
MOTHER... WHERE...?
THE LETTER! IT'S GONE!
WHERE IS ZUKO?!
FWOOM!
FWOOM!

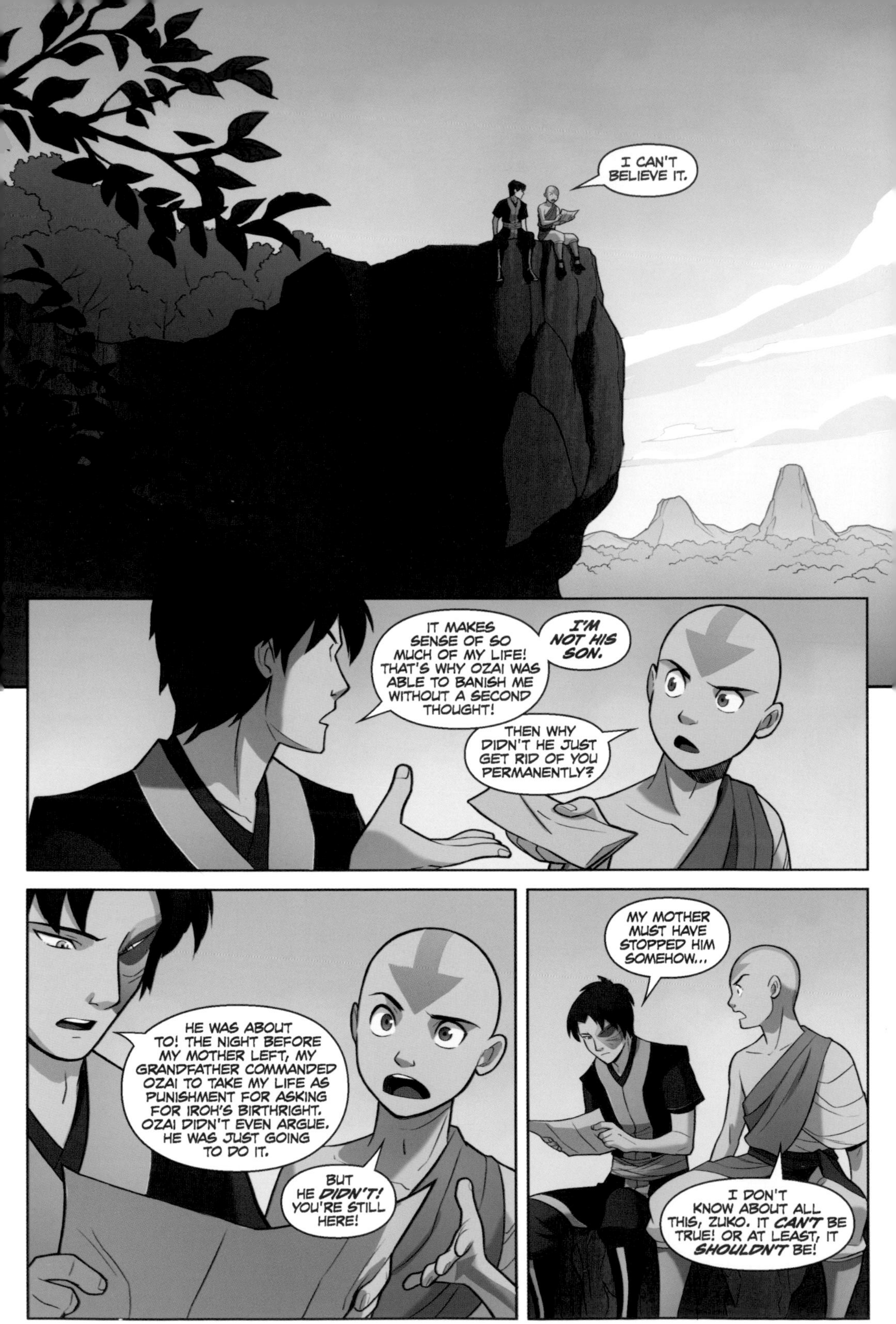
I CAN'T BELIEVE IT.
IT MAKES SENSE OF SO MUCH OF MY LIFE! THAT'S WHY OZAI WAS ABLE TO BANISH ME WITHOUT A SECOND THOUGHT!
I'M NOT HIS SON.
THEN WHY DIDN'T HE JUST GET RID OF YOU PERMANENTLY?
HE WAS ABOUT TO! THE NIGHT BEFORE MY MOTHER LEFT, MY GRANDFATHER COMMANDED OZAI TO TAKE MY LIFE AS PUNISHMENT FOR ASKING FOR IROH'S BIRTHRIGHT. OZAI DIDN'T EVEN ARGUE. HE WAS JUST GOING TO DO IT.
BUT HE DIDN'T! YOU'RE STILL HERE!
MY MOTHER MUST HAVE STOPPED HIM SOMEHOW...
I DON'T KNOW ABOUT ALL THIS, ZUKO. IT CAN'T BE TRUE! OR AT LEAST, IT SHOULDN'T BE!

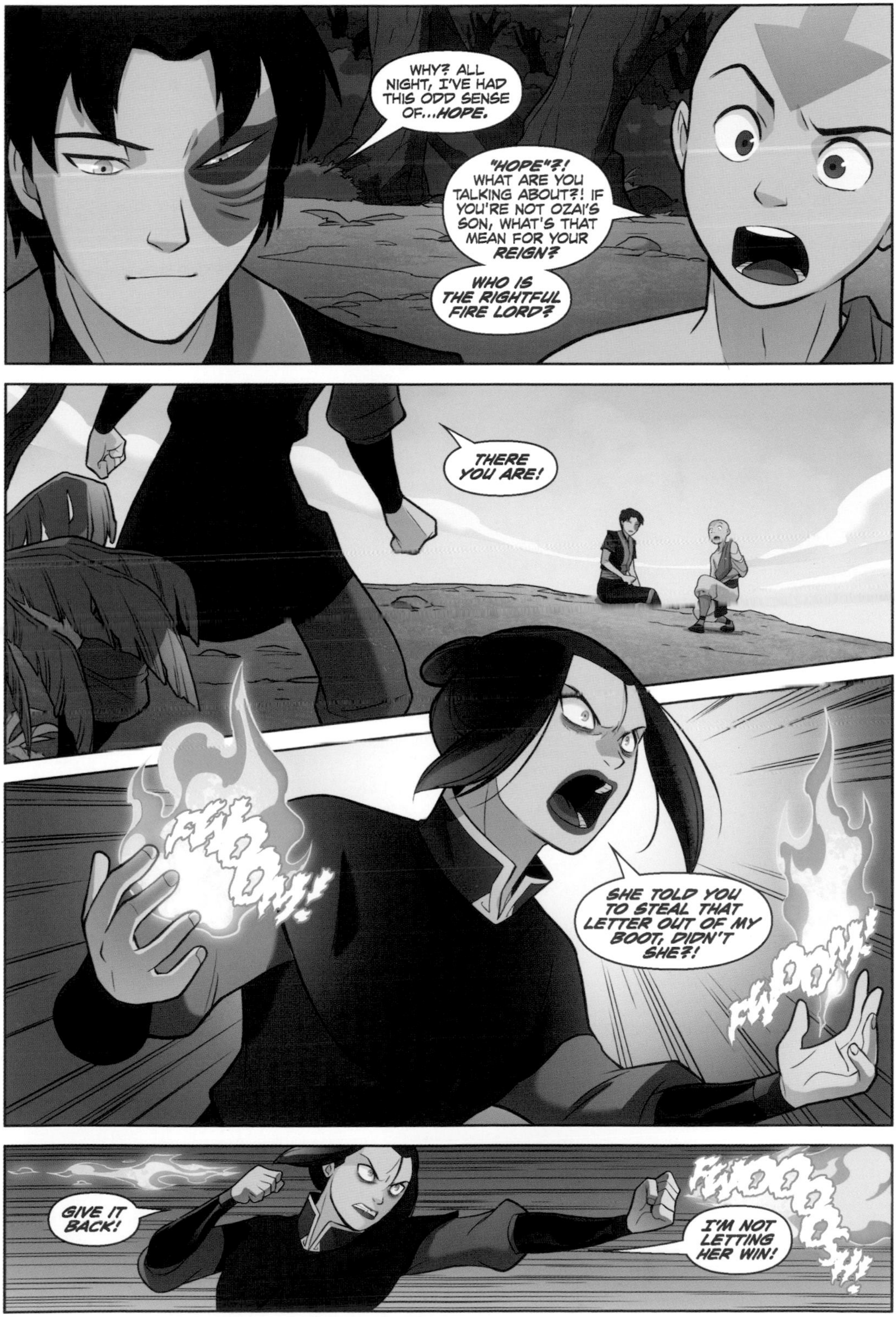
WHY? ALL NIGHT, I'VE HAD THIS ODD SENSE OF...HOPE.
"HOPE"?! WHAT ARE YOU TALKING ABOUT?! IF YOU'RE NOT OZAI'S SON, WHAT'S THAT MEAN FOR YOUR REIGN?
WHO IS THE RIGHTFUL FIRE LORD?
THERE YOU ARE!
FWOOM!
SHE TOLD YOU TO STEAL THAT LETTER OUT OF MY BOOT, DIDN'T SHE?!
FWOOM!
GIVE IT BACK!
I'M NOT LETTING HER WIN!
FWOOOSH!

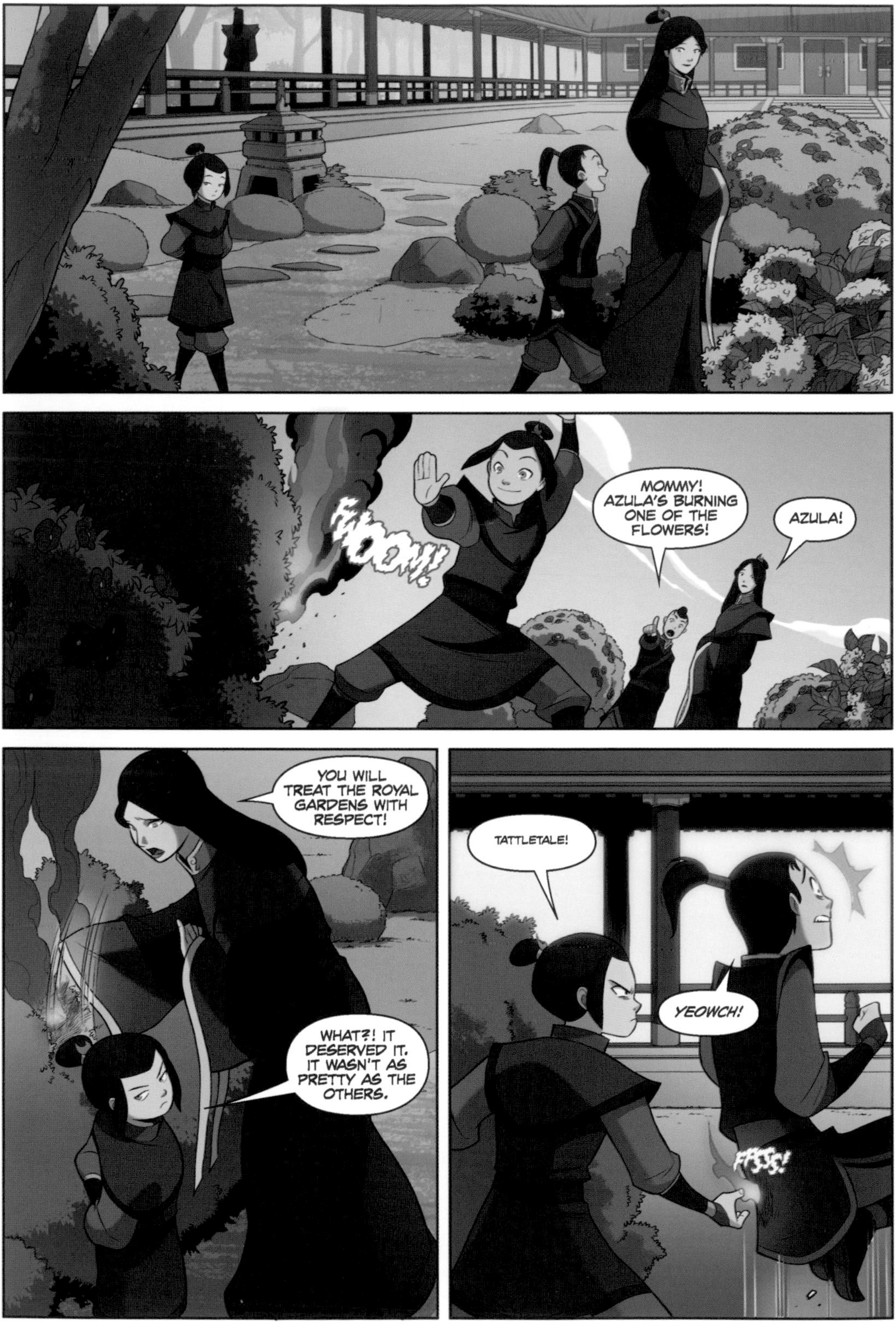
FOOM!
MOMMY! AZULA'S BURNING ONE OF THE FLOWERS!
AZULA!
YOU WILL TREAT THE ROYAL GARDENS WITH RESPECT!
WHAT?! IT DESERVED IT. IT WASN'T AS PRETTY AS THE OTHERS.
TATTLETALE!
YEOWCH!
FSSS!

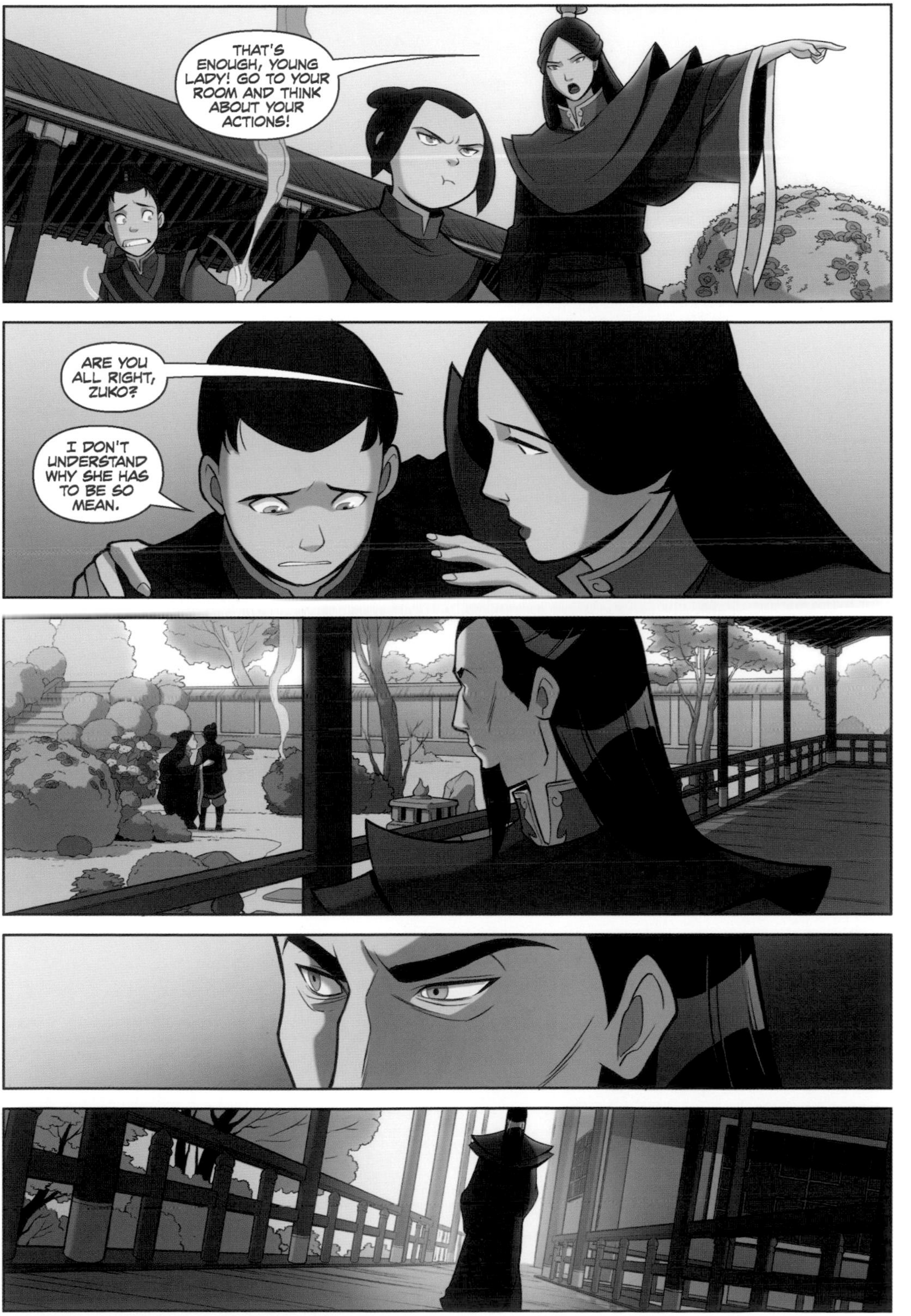
THAT'S ENOUGH, YOUNG LADY! GO TO YOUR ROOM AND THINK ABOUT YOUR ACTIONS!
ARE YOU ALL RIGHT, ZUKO?
I DON'T UNDERSTAND WHY SHE HAS TO BE SO MEAN.

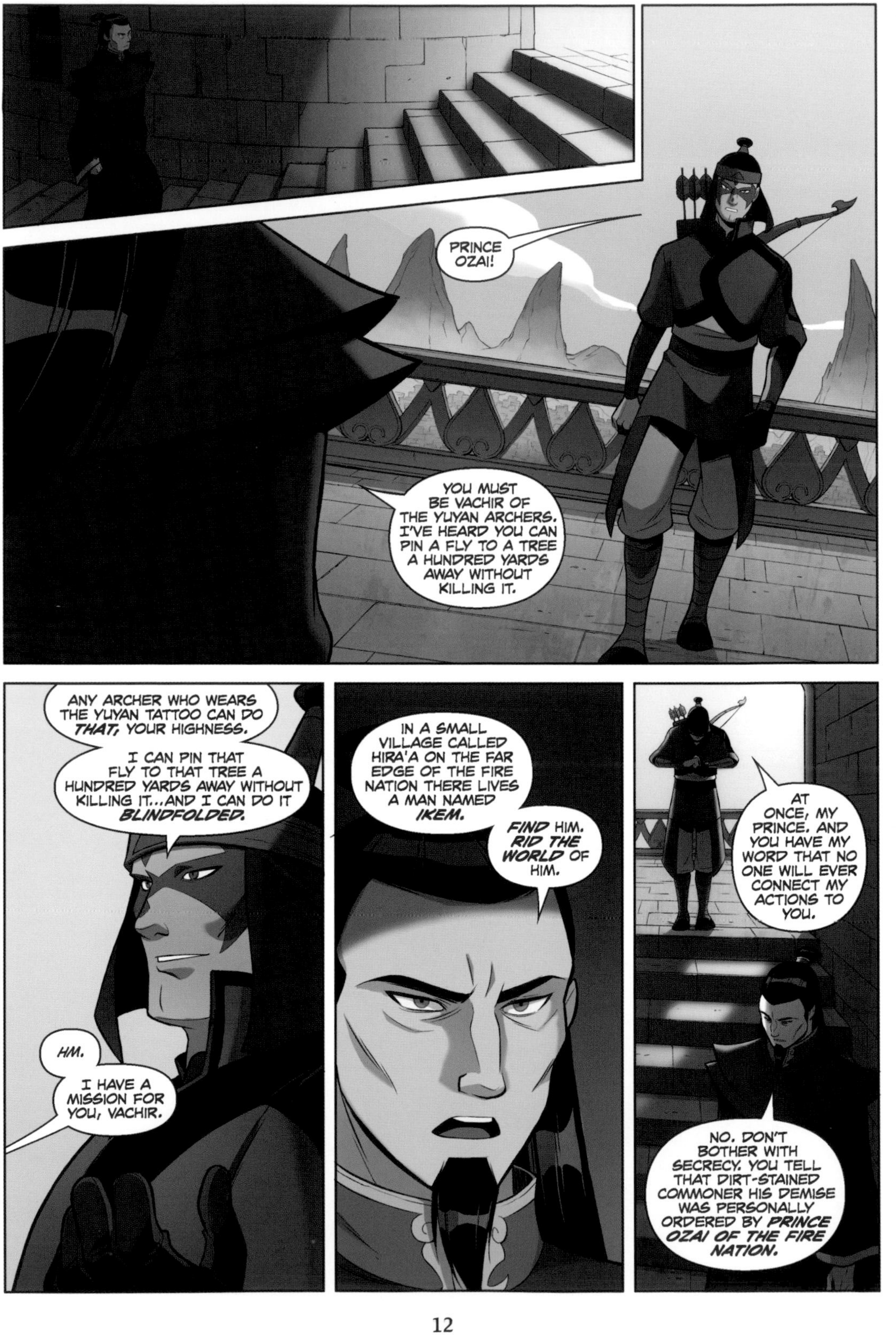
PRINCE OZAI!
YOU MUST BE VACHIR OF THE YUYAN ARCHERS. I'VE HEARD YOU CAN PIN A FLY TO A TREE A HUNDRED YARDS AWAY WITHOUT KILLING IT.
ANY ARCHER WHO WEARS THE YUYAN TATTOO CAN DO *THAT,* YOUR HIGHNESS.
I CAN PIN THAT FLY TO THAT TREE A HUNDRED YARDS AWAY WITHOUT KILLING IT...AND I CAN DO IT *BLINDFOLDED.*
HM.
I HAVE A MISSION FOR YOU, VACHIR.
IN A SMALL VILLAGE CALLED HIRA'A ON THE FAR EDGE OF THE FIRE NATION THERE LIVES A MAN NAMED *IKEM.*
FIND HIM. *RID THE WORLD* OF HIM.
AT ONCE, MY PRINCE. AND YOU HAVE MY WORD THAT NO ONE WILL EVER CONNECT MY ACTIONS TO YOU.
NO. DON'T BOTHER WITH SECRECY. YOU TELL THAT DIRT-STAINED COMMONER HIS DEMISE WAS PERSONALLY ORDERED BY *PRINCE OZAI OF THE FIRE NATION.*

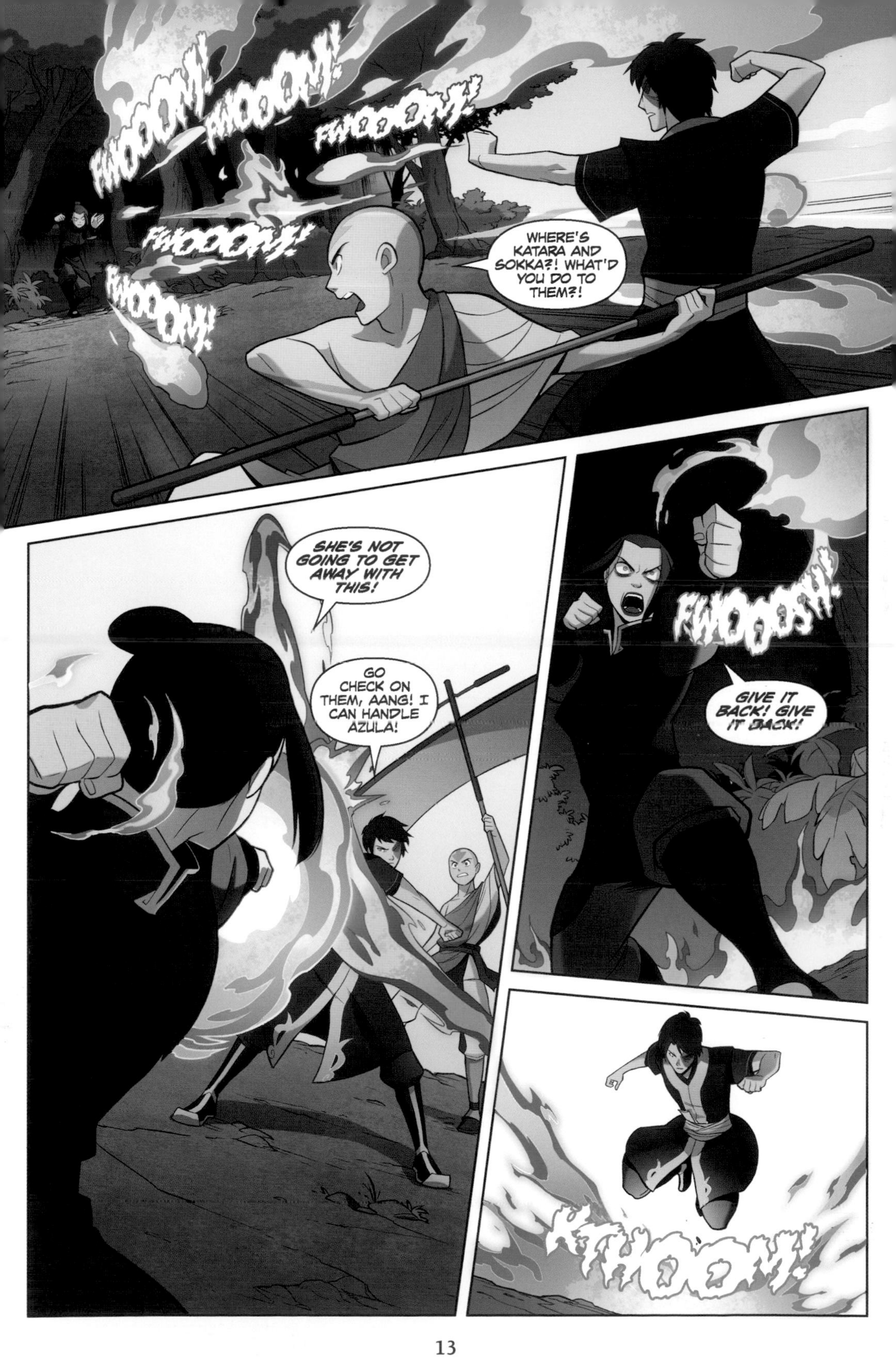
FWOOOM!
FWOOOM!
FWOOOM!
FWOOOM!
FWOOOM!
WHERE'S KATARA AND SOKKA?! WHAT'D YOU DO TO THEM?!
SHE'S NOT GOING TO GET AWAY WITH THIS!
GO CHECK ON THEM, AANG! I CAN HANDLE AZULA!
FWOOOSH!
GIVE IT BACK! GIVE IT BACK!
KTHOOM!

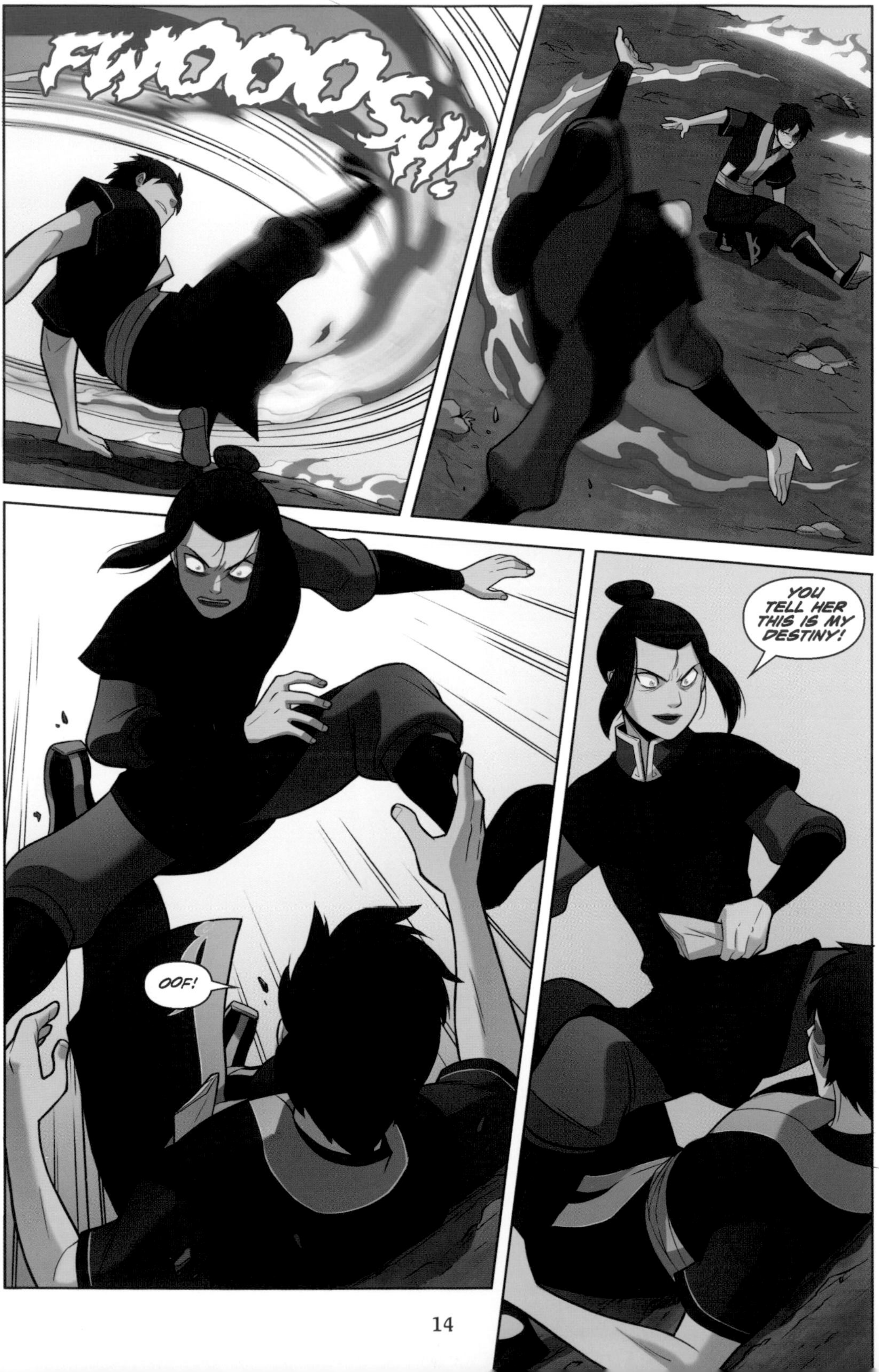
FWOOOSH!
OOF!
YOU TELL HER THIS IS MY DESTINY!

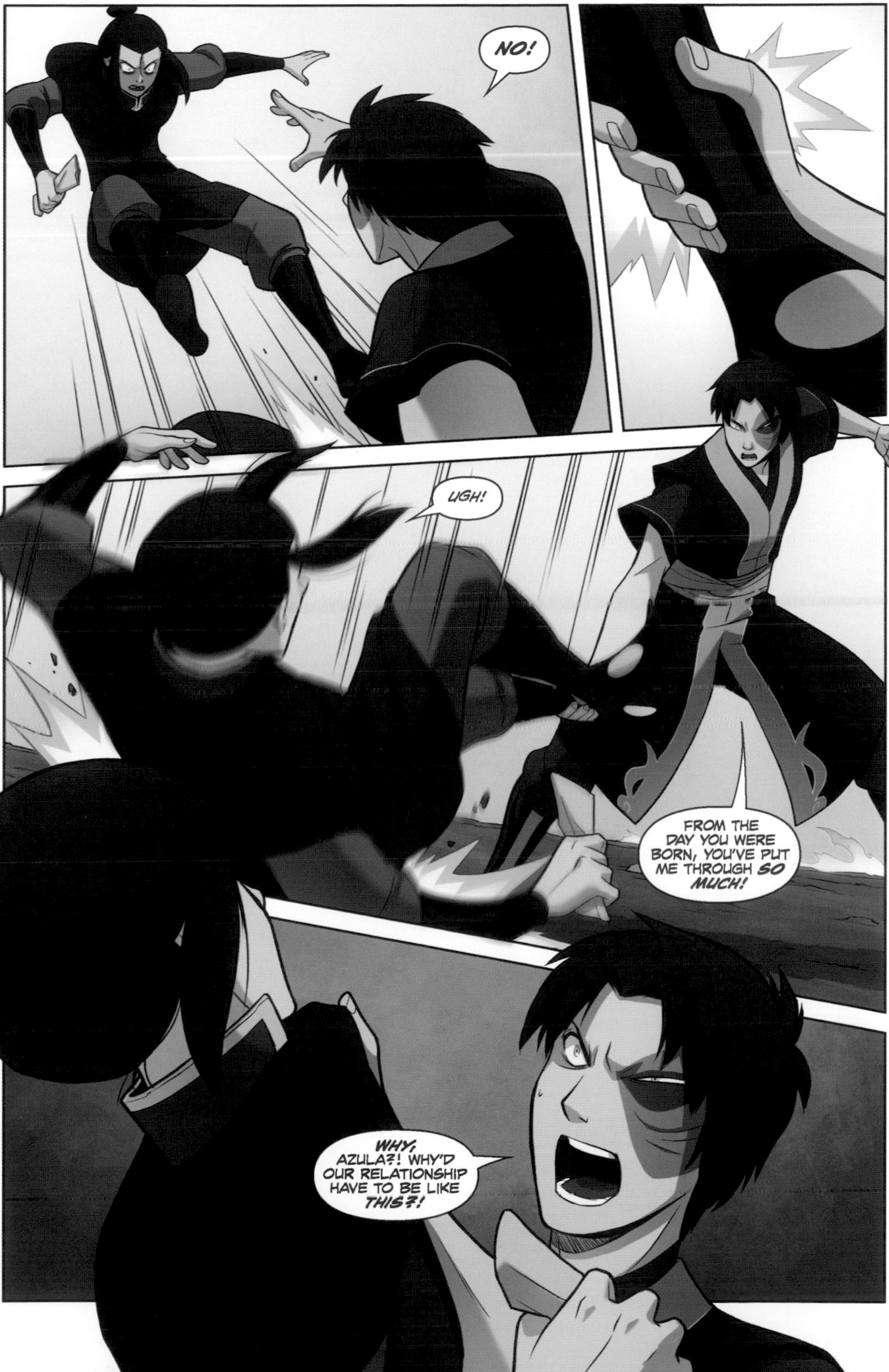
NO!
UGH!
FROM THE DAY YOU WERE BORN, YOU'VE PUT ME THROUGH SO MUCH!
WHY, AZULA?! WHY'D OUR RELATIONSHIP HAVE TO BE LIKE THIS?!

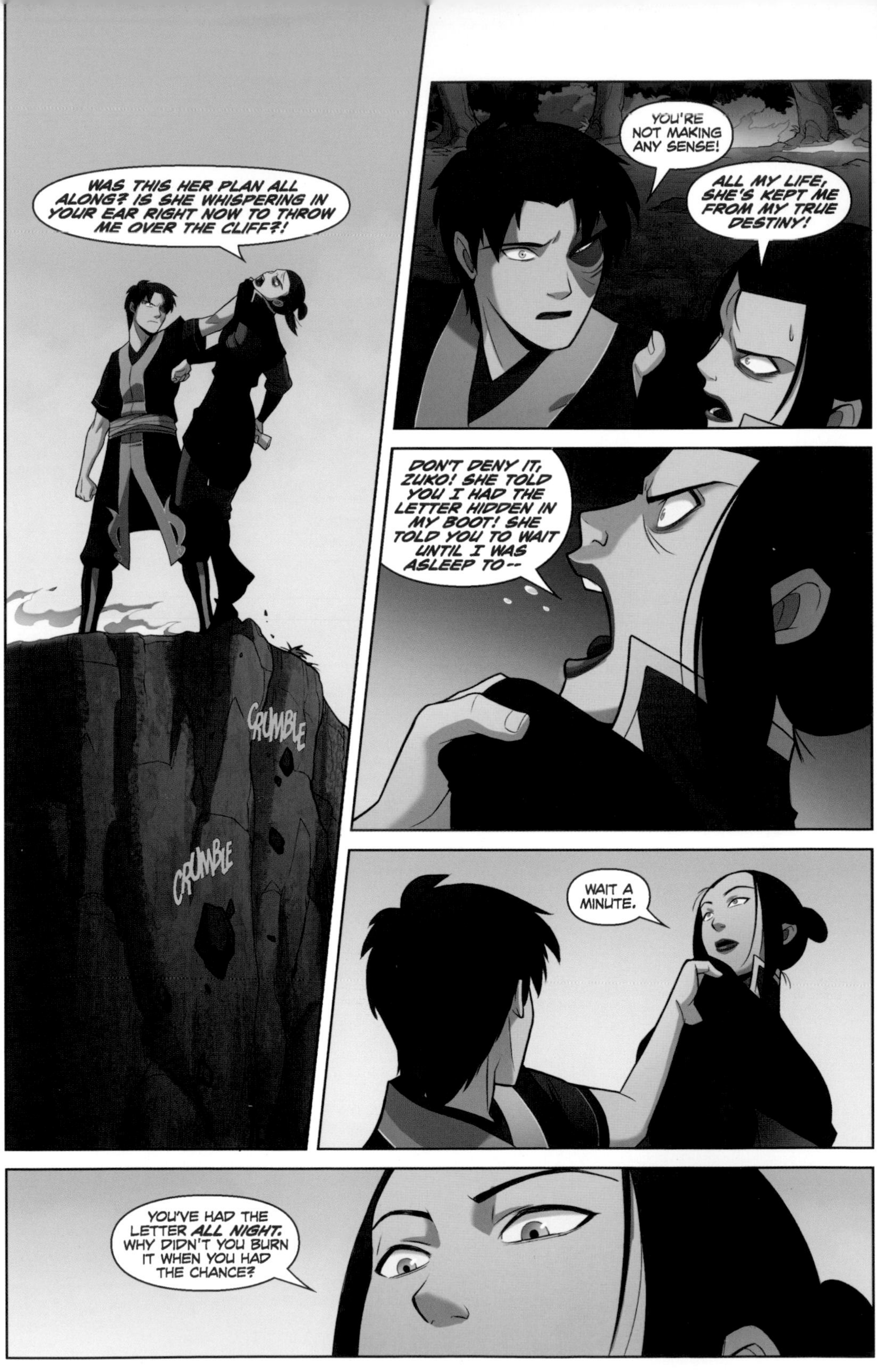
WAS THIS HER PLAN ALL ALONG? IS SHE WHISPERING IN YOUR EAR RIGHT NOW TO THROW ME OVER THE CLIFF?!
CRUMBLE
CRUMBLE
YOU'RE NOT MAKING ANY SENSE!
ALL MY LIFE, SHE'S KEPT ME FROM MY TRUE DESTINY!
DON'T DENY IT, ZUKO! SHE TOLD YOU I HAD THE LETTER HIDDEN IN MY BOOT! SHE TOLD YOU TO WAIT UNTIL I WAS ASLEEP TO--
WAIT A MINUTE.
YOU'VE HAD THE LETTER ALL NIGHT. WHY DIDN'T YOU BURN IT WHEN YOU HAD THE CHANCE?

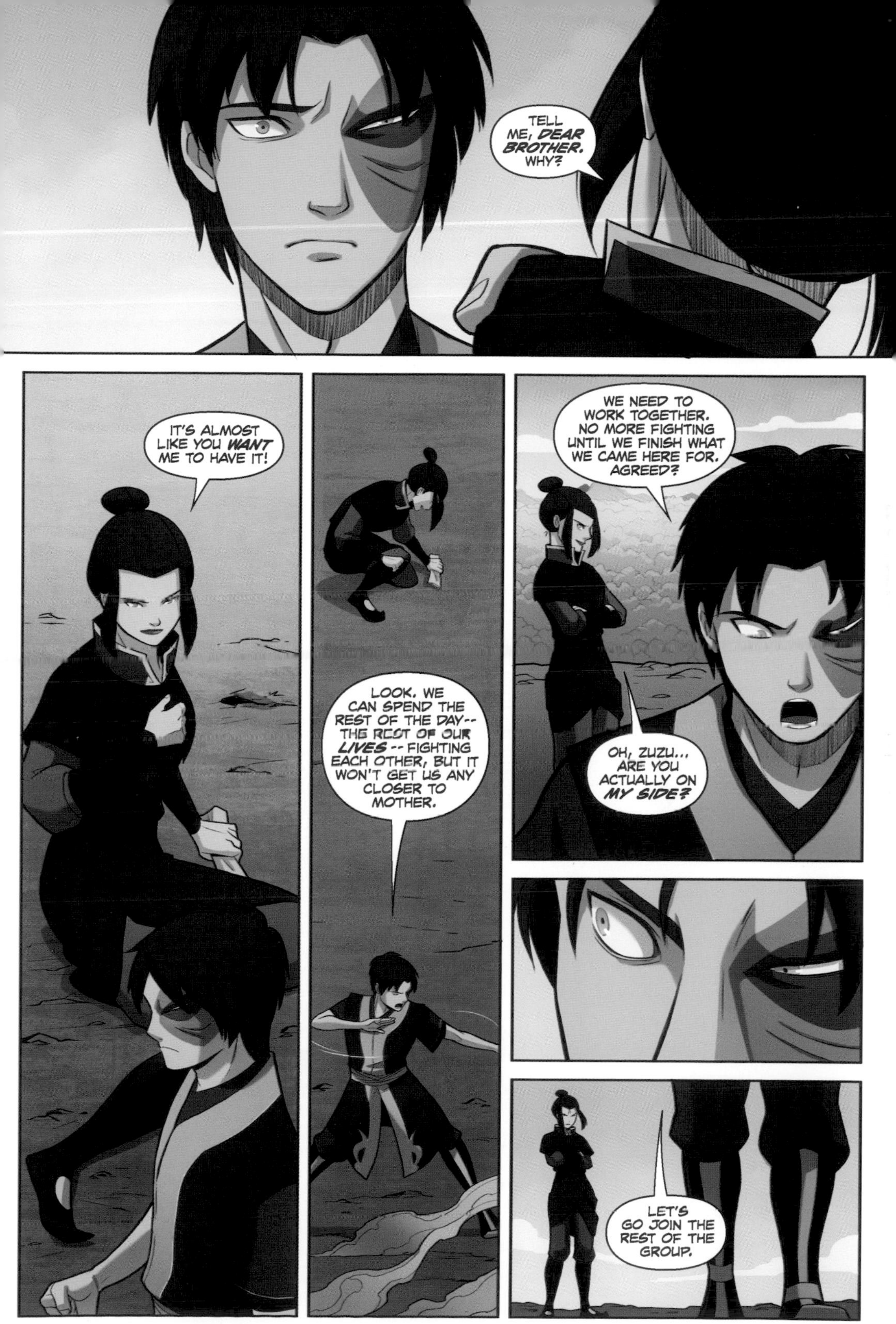

TELL ME, DEAR BROTHER. WHY?
IT'S ALMOST LIKE YOU WANT ME TO HAVE IT!
LOOK. WE CAN SPEND THE REST OF THE DAY-- THE REST OF OUR LIVES -- FIGHTING EACH OTHER, BUT IT WON'T GET US ANY CLOSER TO MOTHER.
WE NEED TO WORK TOGETHER. NO MORE FIGHTING UNTIL WE FINISH WHAT WE CAME HERE FOR. AGREED?
OH, ZUZU... ARE YOU ACTUALLY ON MY SIDE?
LET'S GO JOIN THE REST OF THE GROUP.

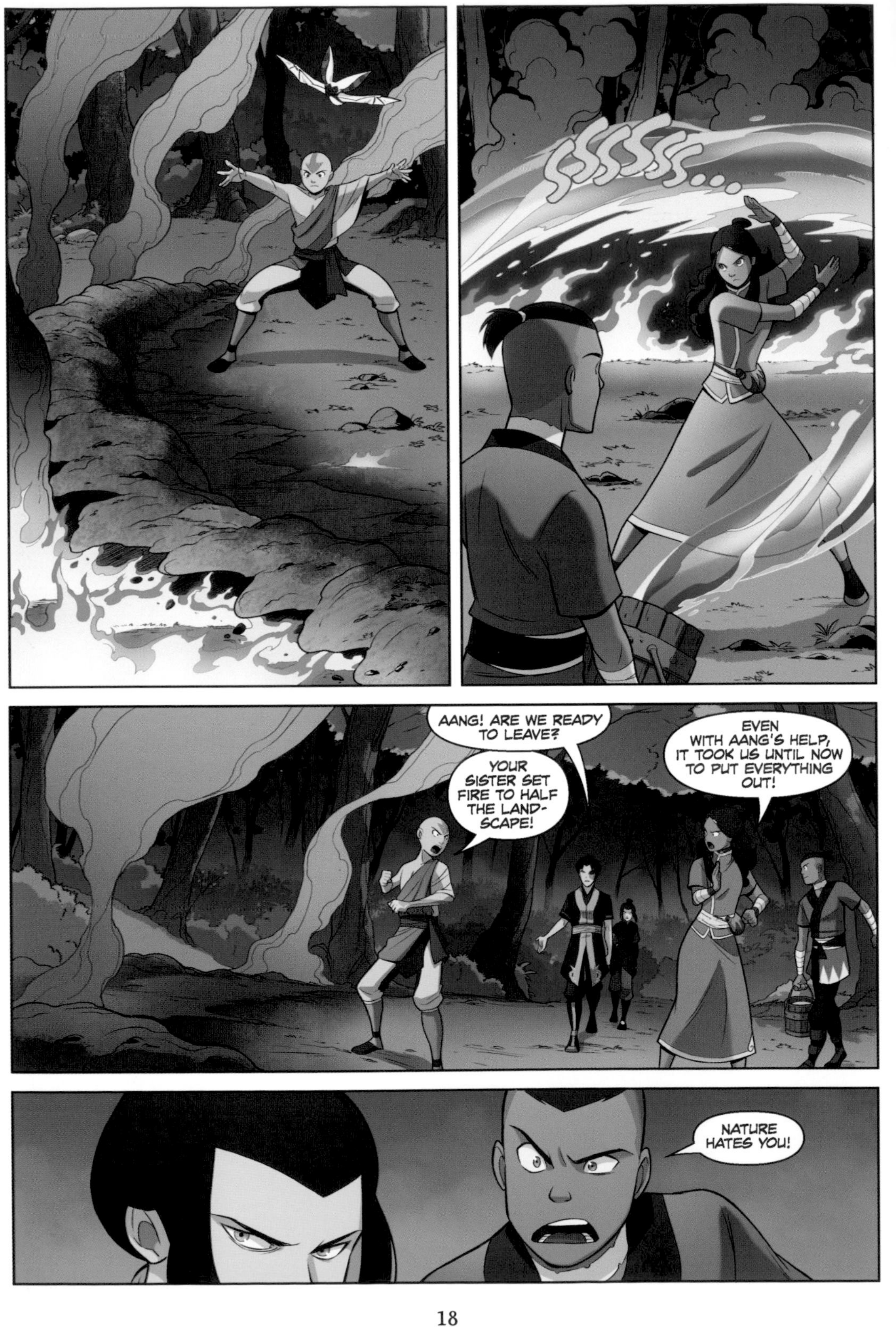
SSSSSS...
AANG! ARE WE READY TO LEAVE?
YOUR SISTER SET FIRE TO HALF THE LAND-SCAPE!
EVEN WITH AANG'S HELP, IT TOOK US UNTIL NOW TO PUT EVERYTHING OUT!
NATURE HATES YOU!

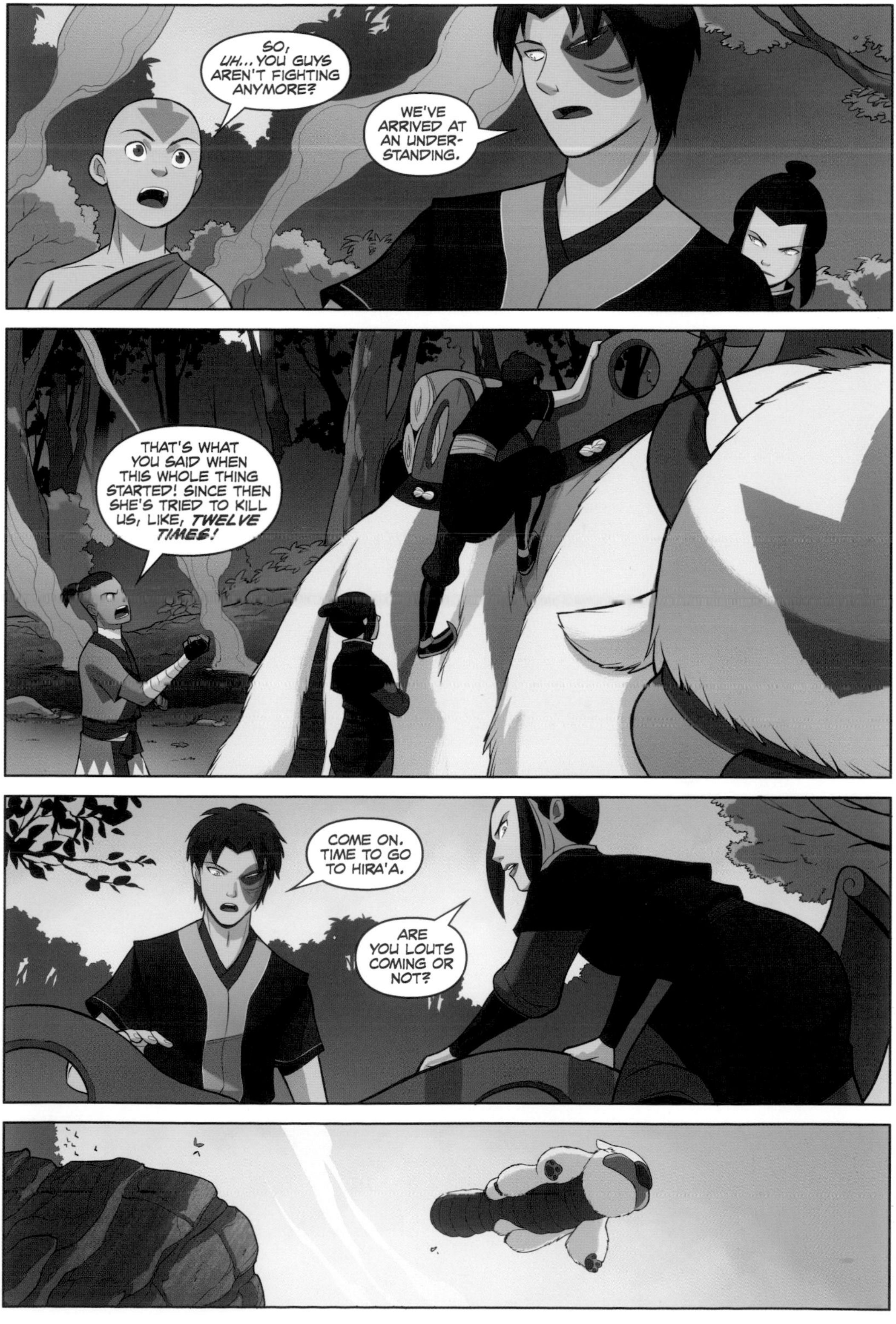
SO, UH...YOU GUYS AREN'T FIGHTING ANYMORE?
WE'VE ARRIVED AT AN UNDER-STANDING.
THAT'S WHAT YOU SAID WHEN THIS WHOLE THING STARTED! SINCE THEN SHE'S TRIED TO KILL US, LIKE, *TWELVE TIMES!*
COME ON. TIME TO GO TO HIRA'A.
ARE YOU LOUTS COMING OR NOT?

DURING TRAINING TODAY, MASTER KUNYO SAID I WAS HOLDING MY ARMS TOO FAR APART FOR ONE OF MY FORMS.

I TOLD HIM THAT'S HOW YOU GET THE BIGGEST FIRE BLAST! HE DIDN'T CARE. HE WANTED ME TO DO THE FORM THE WAY HE DOES IT. THE DUMB WAY.

SO WHEN HE HAD HIS BACK TURNED, I SET HIS PANTS ON FIRE!

HM. YOUR TEACHER SOUNDS LIKE A FOOL. I'LL HAVE HIM SENT TO THE COLONIES.

SERVES HIM RIGHT! WHAT A DUMMY!

HE'S NOT A DUMMY! HE JUST THINKS THAT PROPER FIREBENDING HAS TO START--

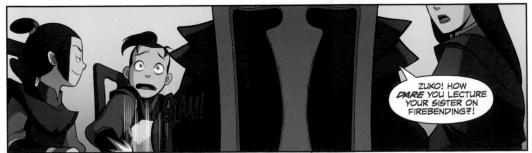

ZUKO! HOW *DARE* YOU LECTURE YOUR SISTER ON FIREBENDING?!

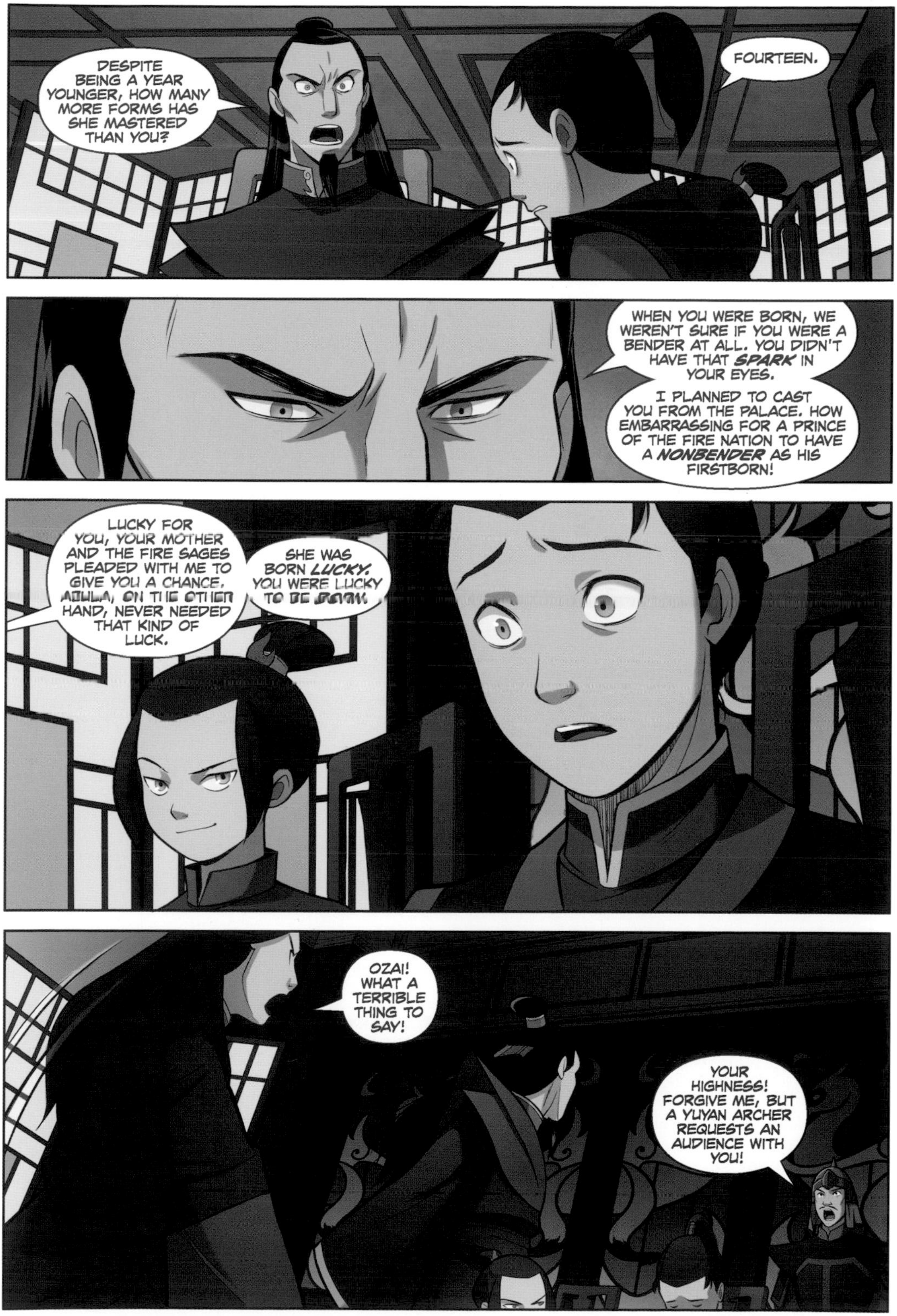
DESPITE BEING A YEAR YOUNGER, HOW MANY MORE FORMS HAS SHE MASTERED THAN YOU?
FOURTEEN.
WHEN YOU WERE BORN, WE WEREN'T SURE IF YOU WERE A BENDER AT ALL. YOU DIDN'T HAVE THAT *SPARK* IN YOUR EYES.
I PLANNED TO CAST YOU FROM THE PALACE. HOW EMBARRASSING FOR A PRINCE OF THE FIRE NATION TO HAVE A *NONBENDER* AS HIS FIRSTBORN!
LUCKY FOR YOU, YOUR MOTHER AND THE FIRE SAGES PLEADED WITH ME TO GIVE YOU A CHANCE. AZULA, ON THE OTHER HAND, NEVER NEEDED THAT KIND OF LUCK.
SHE WAS BORN *LUCKY.* YOU WERE LUCKY TO BE BORN.
OZAI! WHAT A TERRIBLE THING TO SAY!
YOUR HIGHNESS! FORGIVE ME, BUT A YUYAN ARCHER REQUESTS AN AUDIENCE WITH YOU!

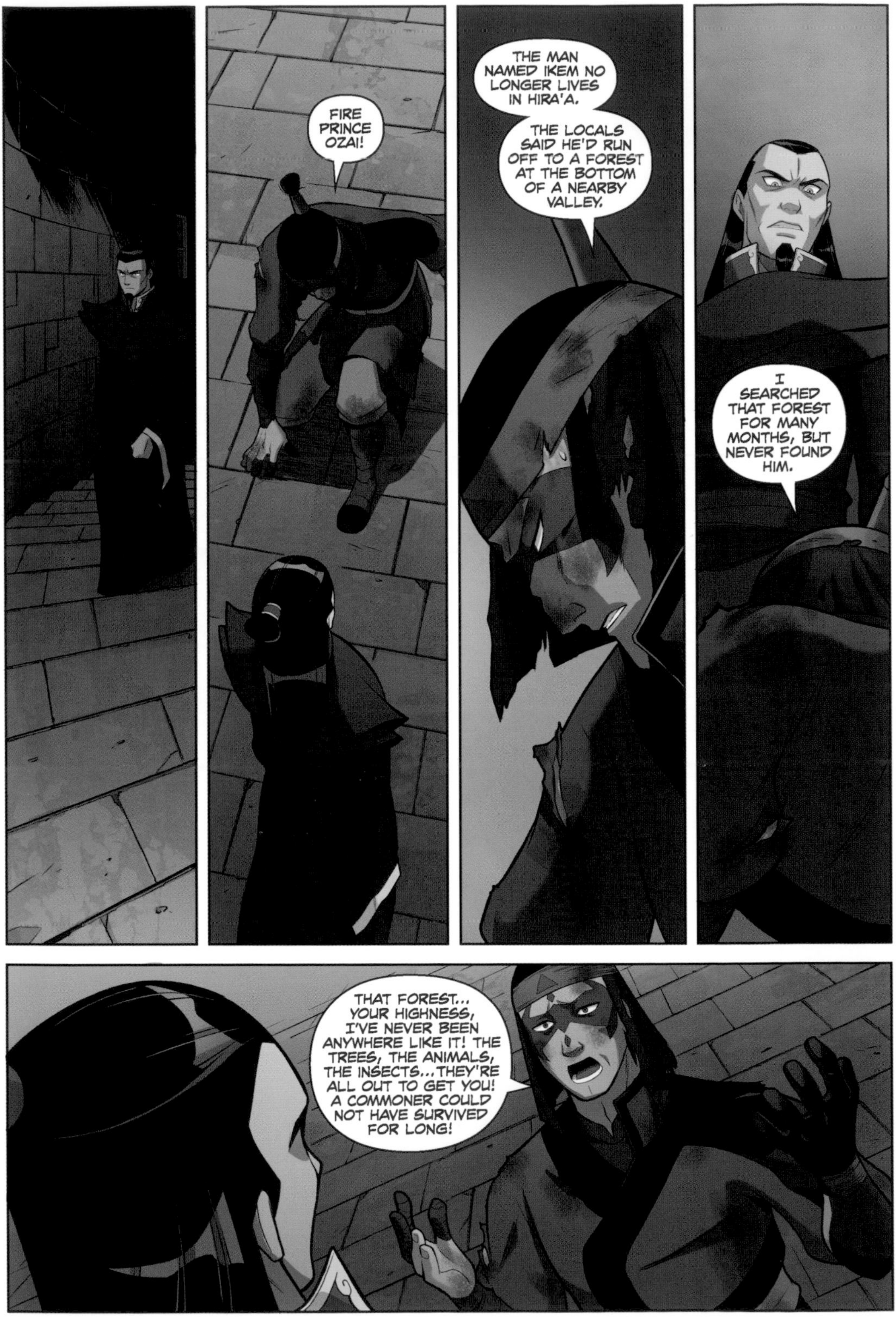
FIRE PRINCE OZAI!
THE MAN NAMED IKEM NO LONGER LIVES IN HIRA'A.
THE LOCALS SAID HE'D RUN OFF TO A FOREST AT THE BOTTOM OF A NEARBY VALLEY.
I SEARCHED THAT FOREST FOR MANY MONTHS, BUT NEVER FOUND HIM.
THAT FOREST... YOUR HIGHNESS, I'VE NEVER BEEN ANYWHERE LIKE IT! THE TREES, THE ANIMALS, THE INSECTS...THEY'RE ALL OUT TO GET YOU! A COMMONER COULD NOT HAVE SURVIVED FOR LONG!

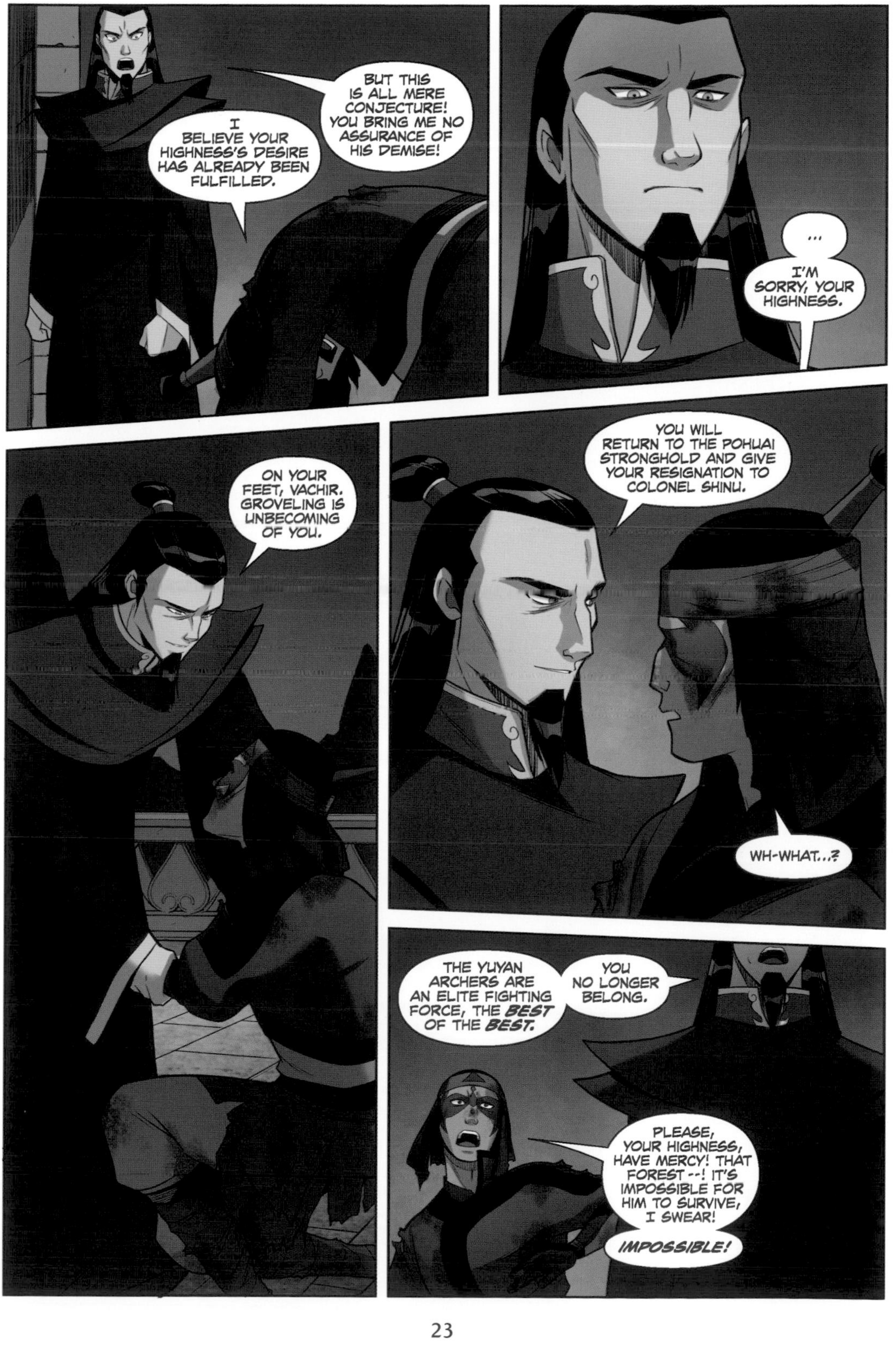
I BELIEVE YOUR HIGHNESS'S DESIRE HAS ALREADY BEEN FULFILLED.
BUT THIS IS ALL MERE CONJECTURE! YOU BRING ME NO ASSURANCE OF HIS DEMISE!
...
I'M SORRY, YOUR HIGHNESS.
ON YOUR FEET, VACHIR. GROVELING IS UNBECOMING OF YOU.
YOU WILL RETURN TO THE POHUAI STRONGHOLD AND GIVE YOUR RESIGNATION TO COLONEL SHINU.
WH-WHAT...?
THE YUYAN ARCHERS ARE AN ELITE FIGHTING FORCE, THE BEST OF THE BEST.
YOU NO LONGER BELONG.
PLEASE, YOUR HIGHNESS, HAVE MERCY! THAT FOREST --! IT'S IMPOSSIBLE FOR HIM TO SURVIVE, I SWEAR!
IMPOSSIBLE!

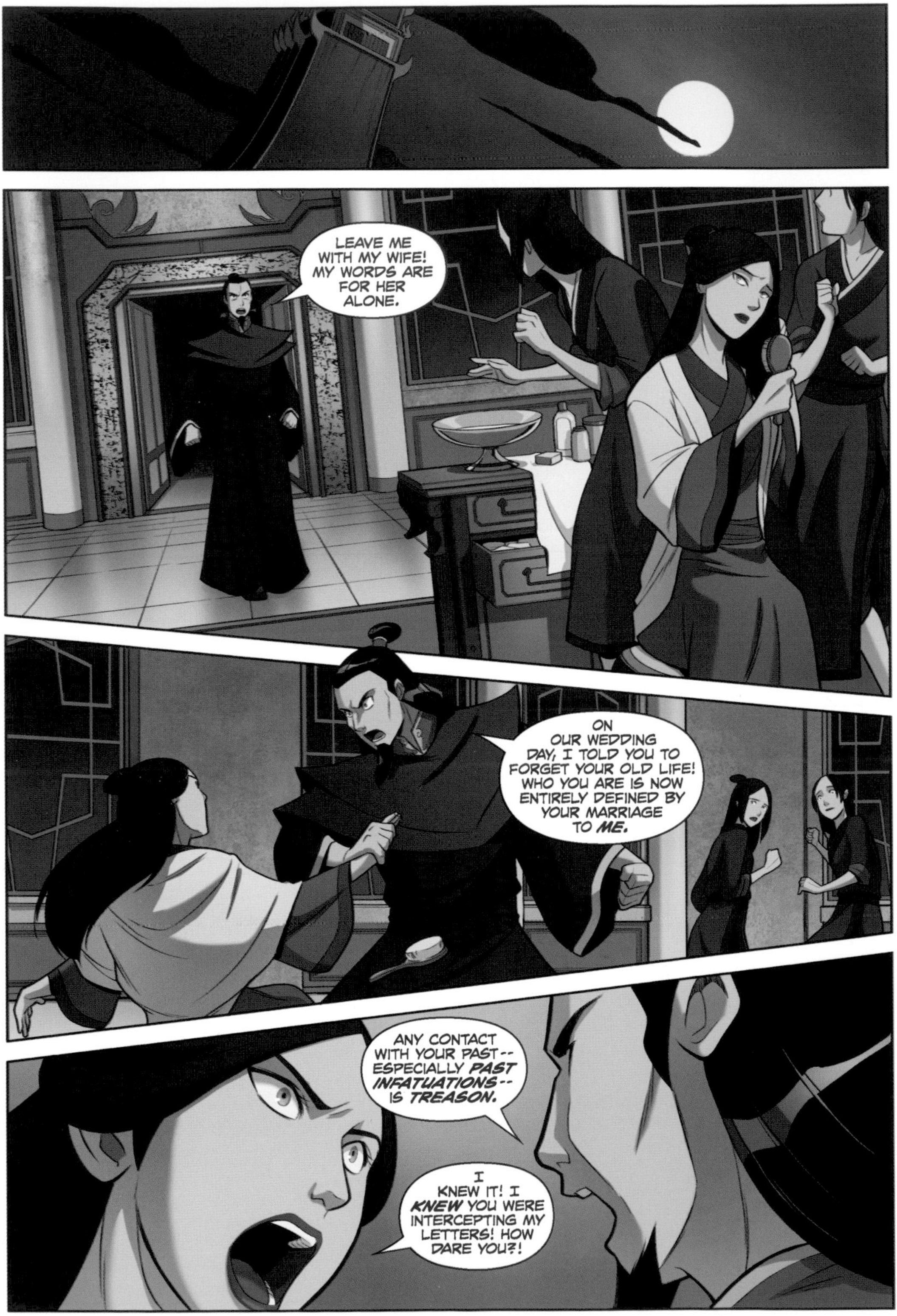
LEAVE ME WITH MY WIFE! MY WORDS ARE FOR HER ALONE.
ON OUR WEDDING DAY, I TOLD YOU TO FORGET YOUR OLD LIFE! WHO YOU ARE IS NOW ENTIRELY DEFINED BY YOUR MARRIAGE TO *ME.*
ANY CONTACT WITH YOUR PAST-- ESPECIALLY *PAST INFATUATIONS*-- IS *TREASON.*
I KNEW IT! I *KNEW* YOU WERE INTERCEPTING MY LETTERS! HOW DARE YOU?!

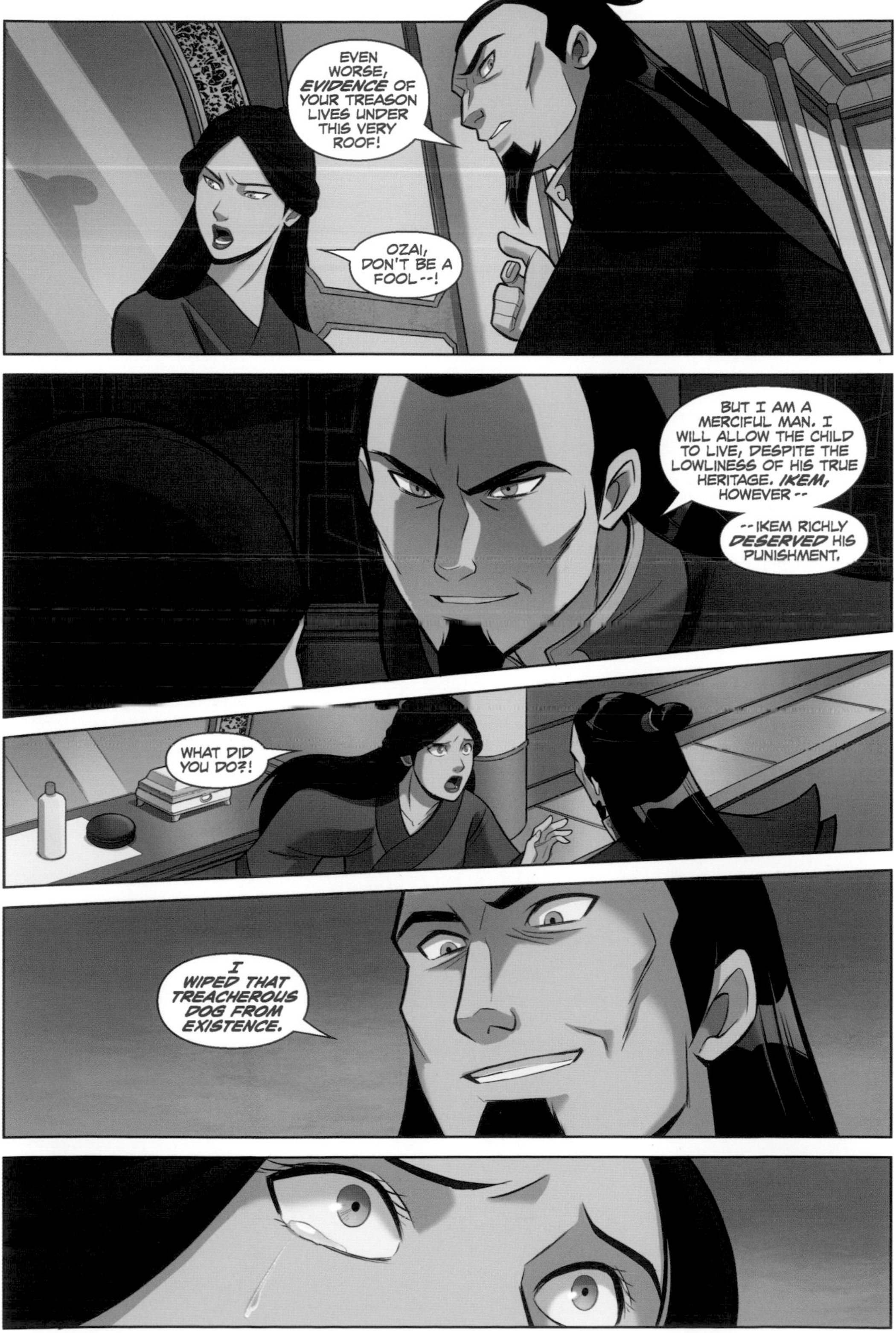
EVEN WORSE, EVIDENCE OF YOUR TREASON LIVES UNDER THIS VERY ROOF!
OZAI, DON'T BE A FOOL--!
BUT I AM A MERCIFUL MAN. I WILL ALLOW THE CHILD TO LIVE, DESPITE THE LOWLINESS OF HIS TRUE HERITAGE. IKEM, HOWEVER--
--IKEM RICHLY DESERVED HIS PUNISHMENT.
WHAT DID YOU DO?!
I WIPED THAT TREACHEROUS DOG FROM EXISTENCE.

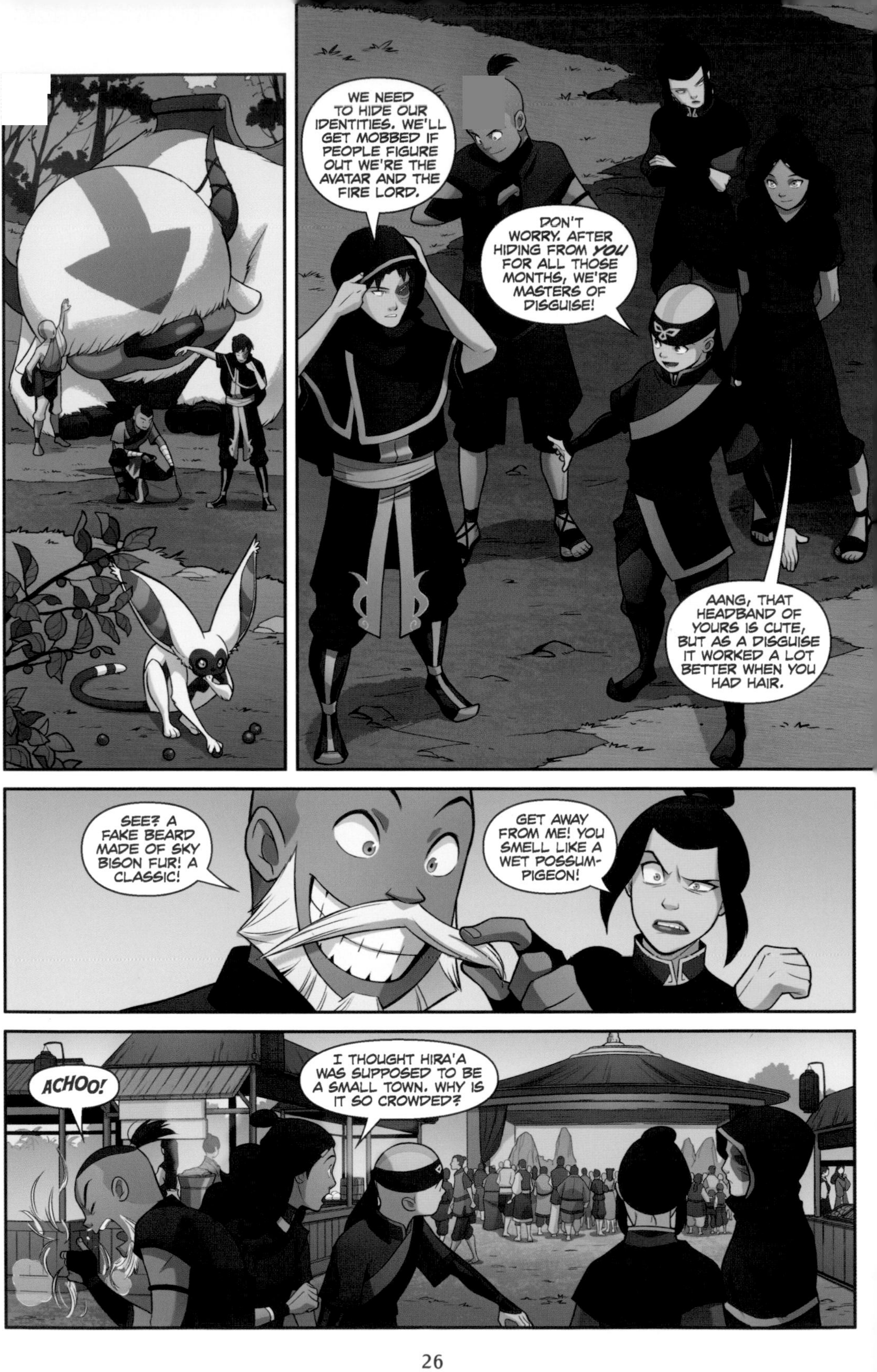
WE NEED TO HIDE OUR IDENTITIES. WE'LL GET MOBBED IF PEOPLE FIGURE OUT WE'RE THE AVATAR AND THE FIRE LORD.
DON'T WORRY. AFTER HIDING FROM *YOU* FOR ALL THOSE MONTHS, WE'RE MASTERS OF DISGUISE!
AANG, THAT HEADBAND OF YOURS IS CUTE, BUT AS A DISGUISE IT WORKED A LOT BETTER WHEN YOU HAD HAIR.
SEE? A FAKE BEARD MADE OF SKY BISON FUR! A CLASSIC!
GET AWAY FROM ME! YOU SMELL LIKE A WET POSSUM-PIGEON!
ACHOO!
I THOUGHT HIRA'A WAS SUPPOSED TO BE A SMALL TOWN. WHY IS IT SO CROWDED?

LOOKS LIKE THEY'RE PERFORMING SOME KIND OF PLAY!

I RECOGNIZE THAT SCENE! IT'S THE FINAL BATTLE IN *LOVE AMONGST DRAGONS*.

WRETCHED WATER SPIRIT! NOW THAT I'VE ESCAPED YOUR CURSE AND REGAINED MY TRUE NATURE, YOU SHALL PAY FOR YOUR TRICKERY!

HAVE YOU LEARNED NOTHING FROM YOUR TIME AMONGST THE MORTALS? BY THREATENING ME, YOU INVITE YOUR OWN DOOM!

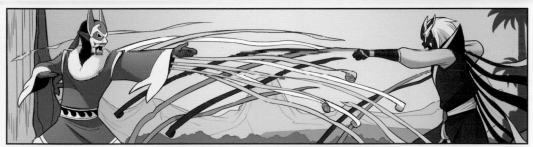

NOOO! CURSE YOU, FOUL DRAGON!

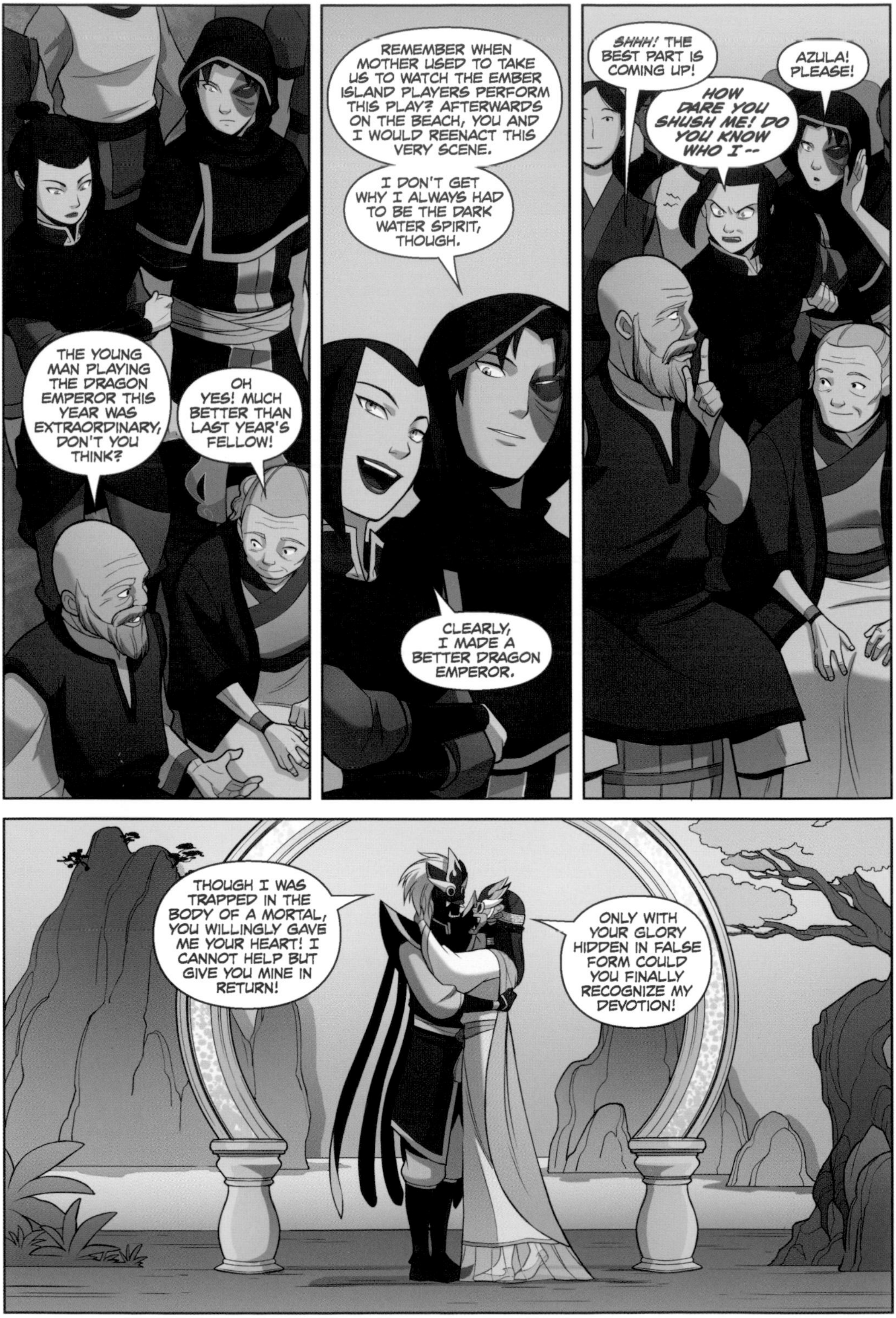
THE YOUNG MAN PLAYING THE DRAGON EMPEROR THIS YEAR WAS EXTRAORDINARY, DON'T YOU THINK?
OH YES! MUCH BETTER THAN LAST YEAR'S FELLOW!
REMEMBER WHEN MOTHER USED TO TAKE US TO WATCH THE EMBER ISLAND PLAYERS PERFORM THIS PLAY? AFTERWARDS ON THE BEACH, YOU AND I WOULD REENACT THIS VERY SCENE.
I DON'T GET WHY I ALWAYS HAD TO BE THE DARK WATER SPIRIT, THOUGH.
CLEARLY, I MADE A BETTER DRAGON EMPEROR.
SHHH! THE BEST PART IS COMING UP!
HOW DARE YOU SHUSH ME! DO YOU KNOW WHO I --
AZULA! PLEASE!
THOUGH I WAS TRAPPED IN THE BODY OF A MORTAL, YOU WILLINGLY GAVE ME YOUR HEART! I CANNOT HELP BUT GIVE YOU MINE IN RETURN!
ONLY WITH YOUR GLORY HIDDEN IN FALSE FORM COULD YOU FINALLY RECOGNIZE MY DEVOTION!

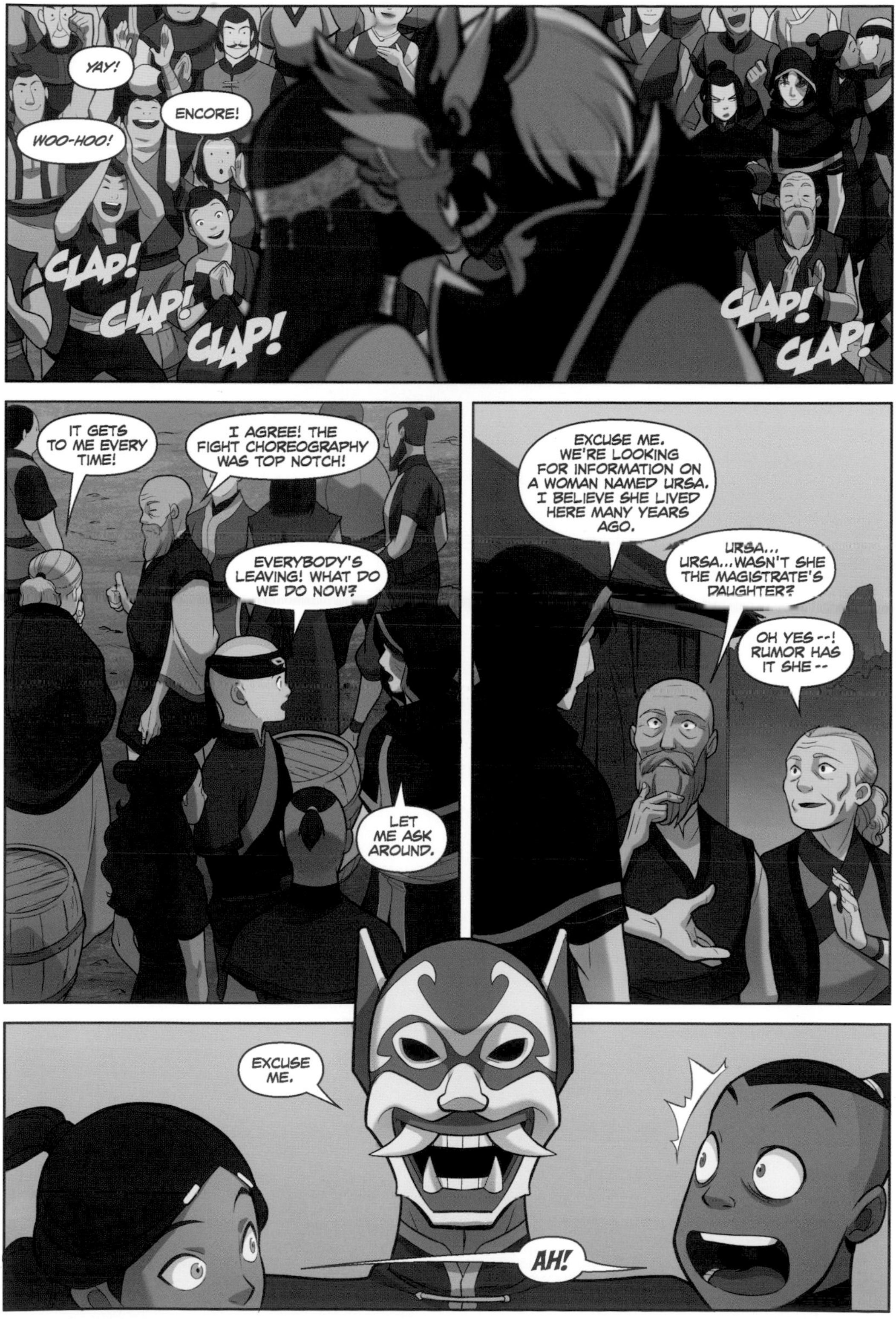
YAY!
ENCORE!
WOO-HOO!
CLAP! CLAP! CLAP!
CLAP! CLAP!
IT GETS TO ME EVERY TIME!
I AGREE! THE FIGHT CHOREOGRAPHY WAS TOP NOTCH!
EVERYBODY'S LEAVING! WHAT DO WE DO NOW?
LET ME ASK AROUND.
EXCUSE ME. WE'RE LOOKING FOR INFORMATION ON A WOMAN NAMED URSA. I BELIEVE SHE LIVED HERE MANY YEARS AGO.
URSA... URSA...WASN'T SHE THE MAGISTRATE'S DAUGHTER?
OH YES --! RUMOR HAS IT SHE --
EXCUSE ME.
AH!

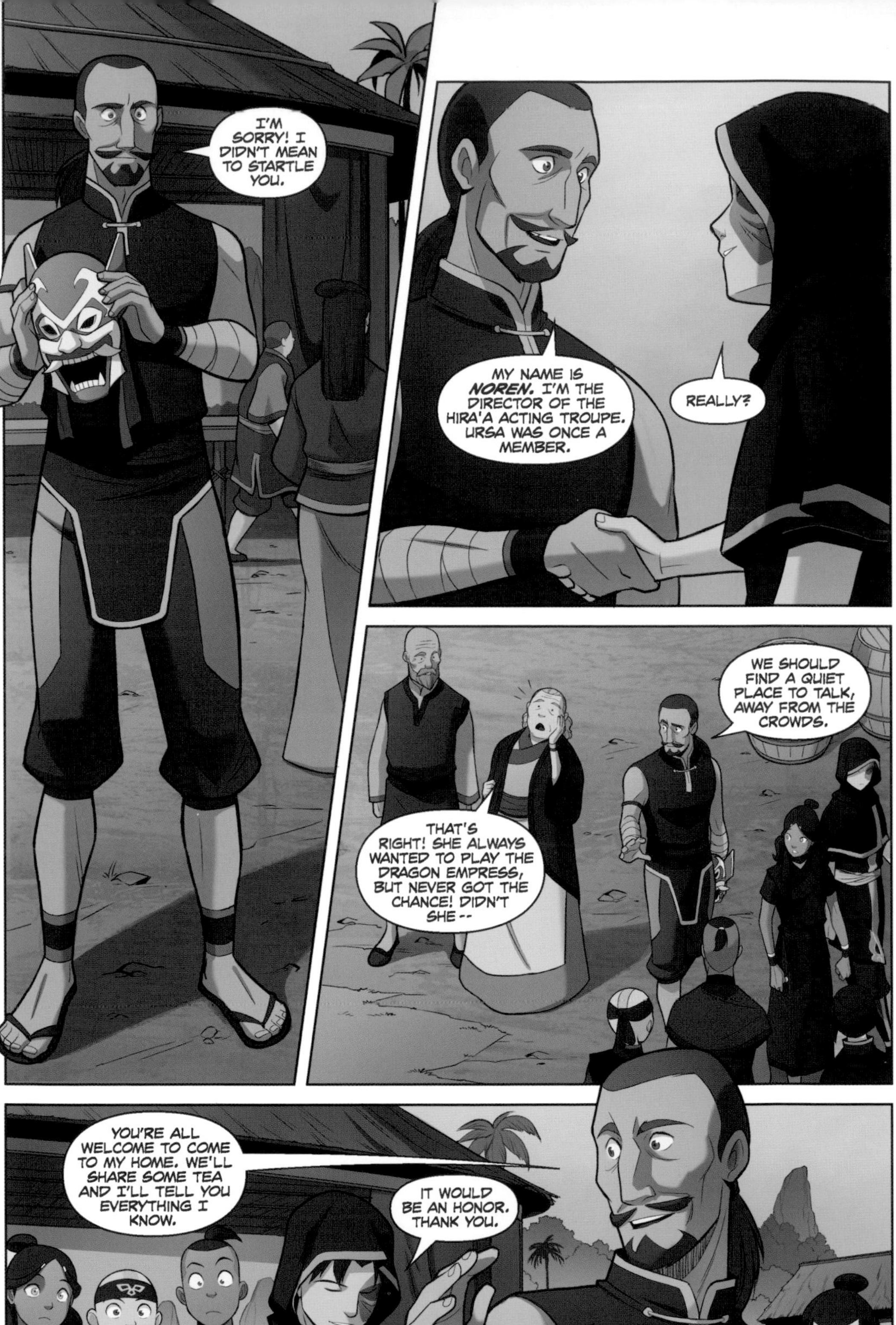

I'M SORRY! I DIDN'T MEAN TO STARTLE YOU.
MY NAME IS NOREN. I'M THE DIRECTOR OF THE HIRA'A ACTING TROUPE. URSA WAS ONCE A MEMBER.
REALLY?
WE SHOULD FIND A QUIET PLACE TO TALK, AWAY FROM THE CROWDS.
THAT'S RIGHT! SHE ALWAYS WANTED TO PLAY THE DRAGON EMPRESS, BUT NEVER GOT THE CHANCE! DIDN'T SHE --
YOU'RE ALL WELCOME TO COME TO MY HOME. WE'LL SHARE SOME TEA AND I'LL TELL YOU EVERYTHING I KNOW.
IT WOULD BE AN HONOR. THANK YOU.

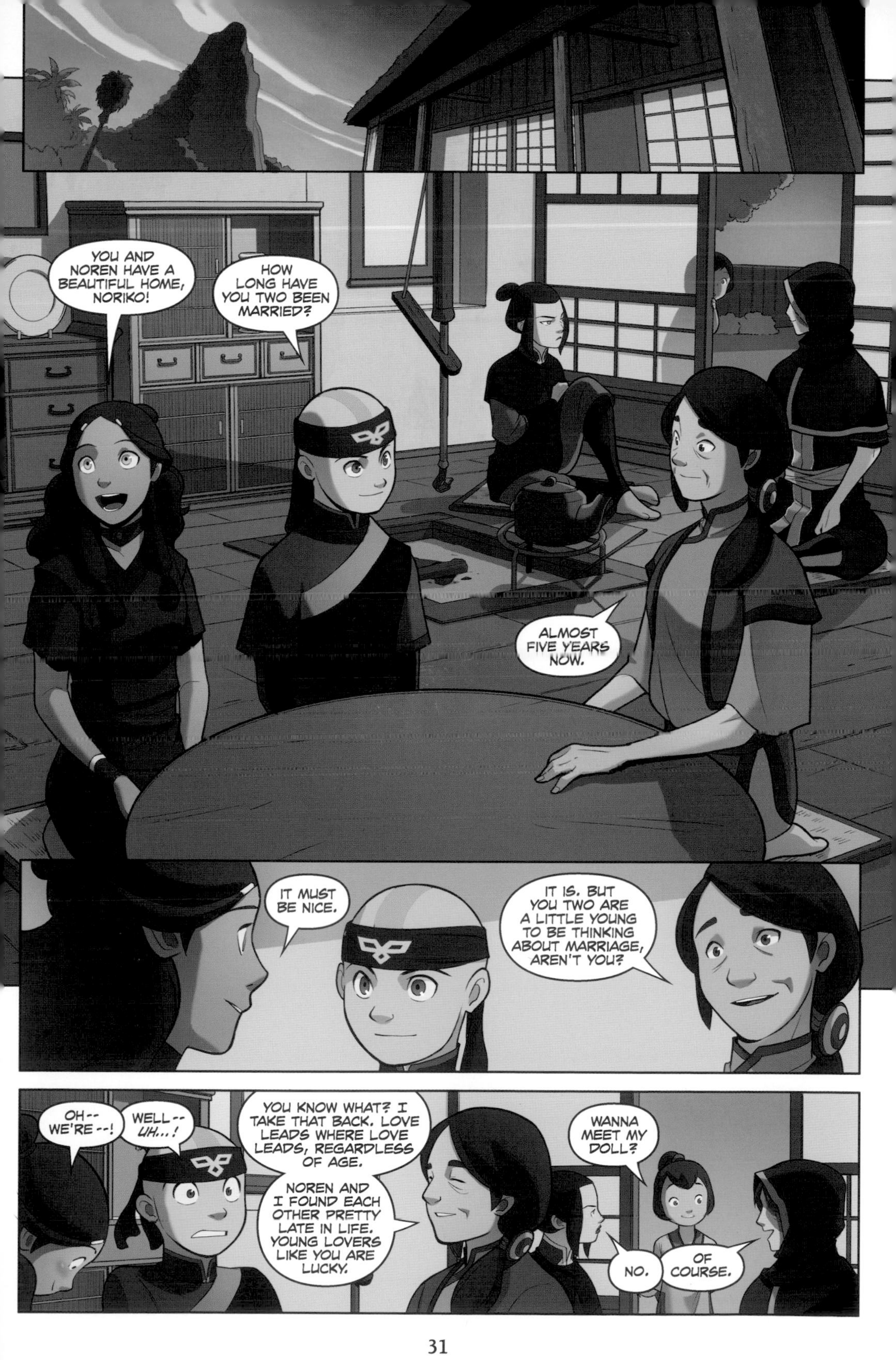
YOU AND NOREN HAVE A BEAUTIFUL HOME, NORIKO!
HOW LONG HAVE YOU TWO BEEN MARRIED?
ALMOST FIVE YEARS NOW.
IT MUST BE NICE.
IT IS. BUT YOU TWO ARE A LITTLE YOUNG TO BE THINKING ABOUT MARRIAGE, AREN'T YOU?
OH-- WE'RE--!
WELL-- *UH...!*
YOU KNOW WHAT? I TAKE THAT BACK. LOVE LEADS WHERE LOVE LEADS, REGARDLESS OF AGE.
NOREN AND I FOUND EACH OTHER PRETTY LATE IN LIFE. YOUNG LOVERS LIKE YOU ARE LUCKY.
WANNA MEET MY DOLL?
NO.
OF COURSE.

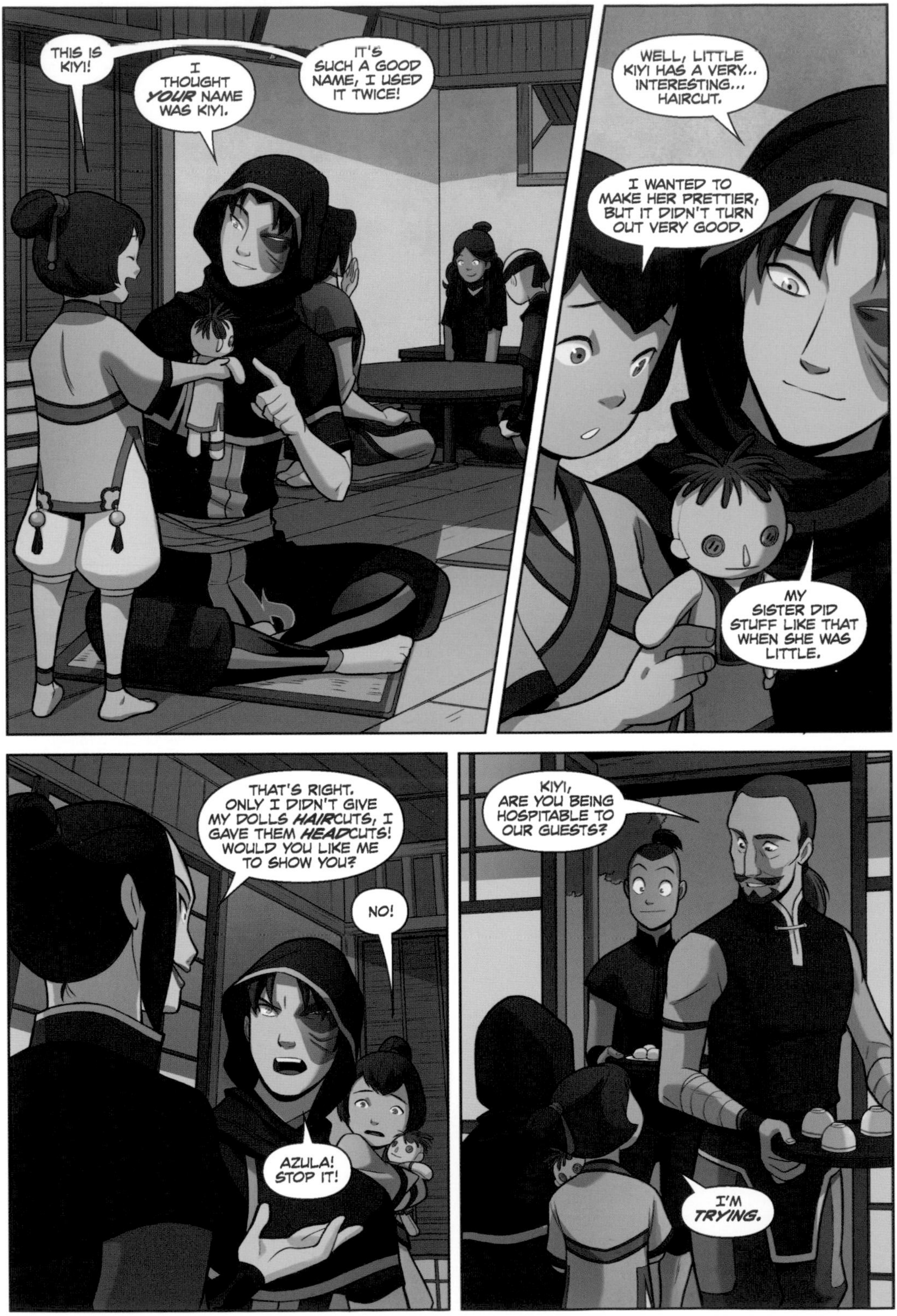
THIS IS KIYI!
I THOUGHT YOUR NAME WAS KIYI.
IT'S SUCH A GOOD NAME, I USED IT TWICE!
WELL, LITTLE KIYI HAS A VERY... INTERESTING... HAIRCUT.
I WANTED TO MAKE HER PRETTIER, BUT IT DIDN'T TURN OUT VERY GOOD.
MY SISTER DID STUFF LIKE THAT WHEN SHE WAS LITTLE.
THAT'S RIGHT. ONLY I DIDN'T GIVE MY DOLLS HAIRCUTS, I GAVE THEM HEADCUTS! WOULD YOU LIKE ME TO SHOW YOU?
NO!
AZULA! STOP IT!
KIYI, ARE YOU BEING HOSPITABLE TO OUR GUESTS?
I'M TRYING.

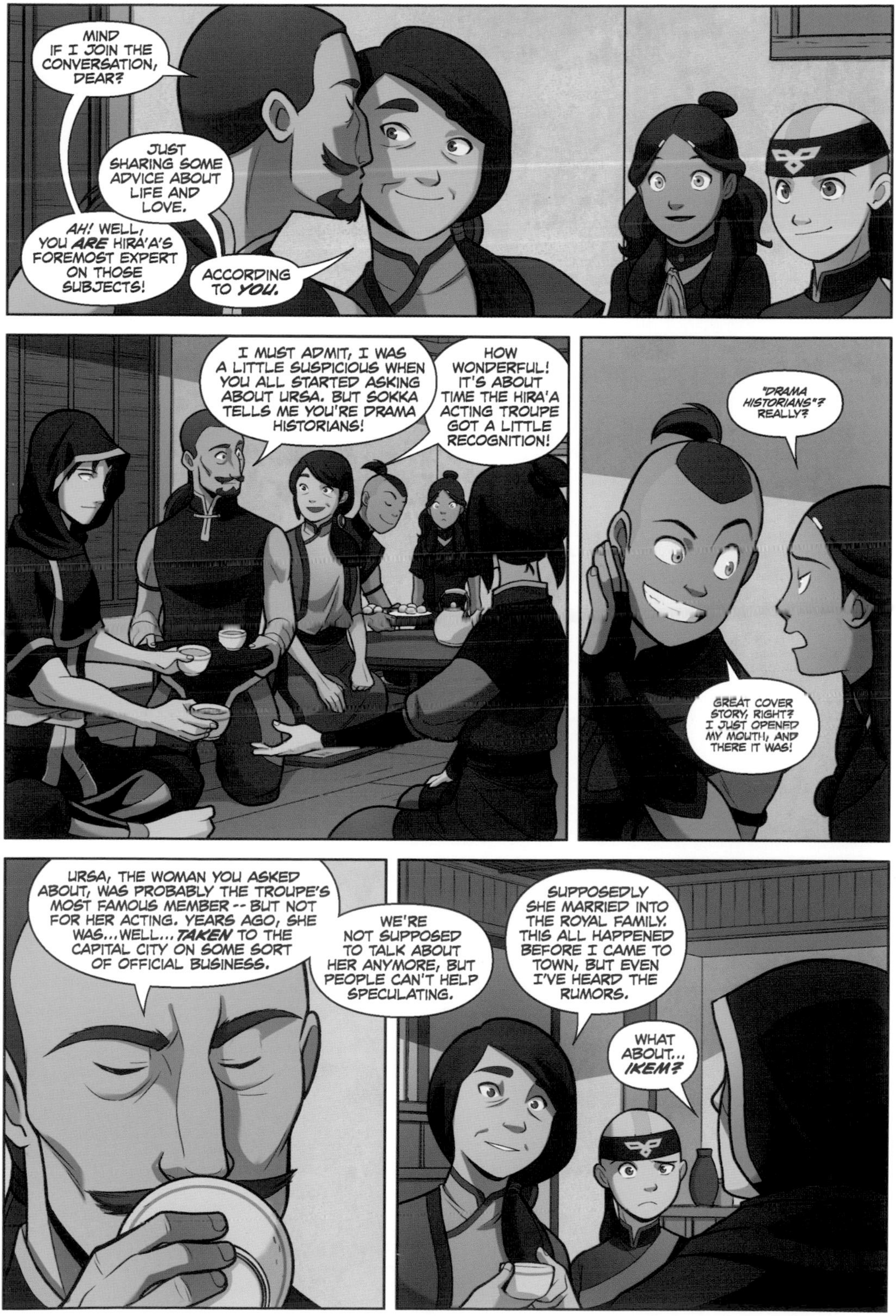
MIND IF I JOIN THE CONVERSATION, DEAR?
JUST SHARING SOME ADVICE ABOUT LIFE AND LOVE.
AH! WELL, YOU ARE HIRA'A'S FOREMOST EXPERT ON THOSE SUBJECTS!
ACCORDING TO YOU.
I MUST ADMIT, I WAS A LITTLE SUSPICIOUS WHEN YOU ALL STARTED ASKING ABOUT URSA. BUT SOKKA TELLS ME YOU'RE DRAMA HISTORIANS!
HOW WONDERFUL! IT'S ABOUT TIME THE HIRA'A ACTING TROUPE GOT A LITTLE RECOGNITION!
"DRAMA HISTORIANS"? REALLY?
GREAT COVER STORY, RIGHT? I JUST OPENED MY MOUTH, AND THERE IT WAS!
URSA, THE WOMAN YOU ASKED ABOUT, WAS PROBABLY THE TROUPE'S MOST FAMOUS MEMBER -- BUT NOT FOR HER ACTING. YEARS AGO, SHE WAS... WELL... TAKEN TO THE CAPITAL CITY ON SOME SORT OF OFFICIAL BUSINESS.
WE'RE NOT SUPPOSED TO TALK ABOUT HER ANYMORE, BUT PEOPLE CAN'T HELP SPECULATING.
SUPPOSEDLY SHE MARRIED INTO THE ROYAL FAMILY. THIS ALL HAPPENED BEFORE I CAME TO TOWN, BUT EVEN I'VE HEARD THE RUMORS.
WHAT ABOUT... IKEM?

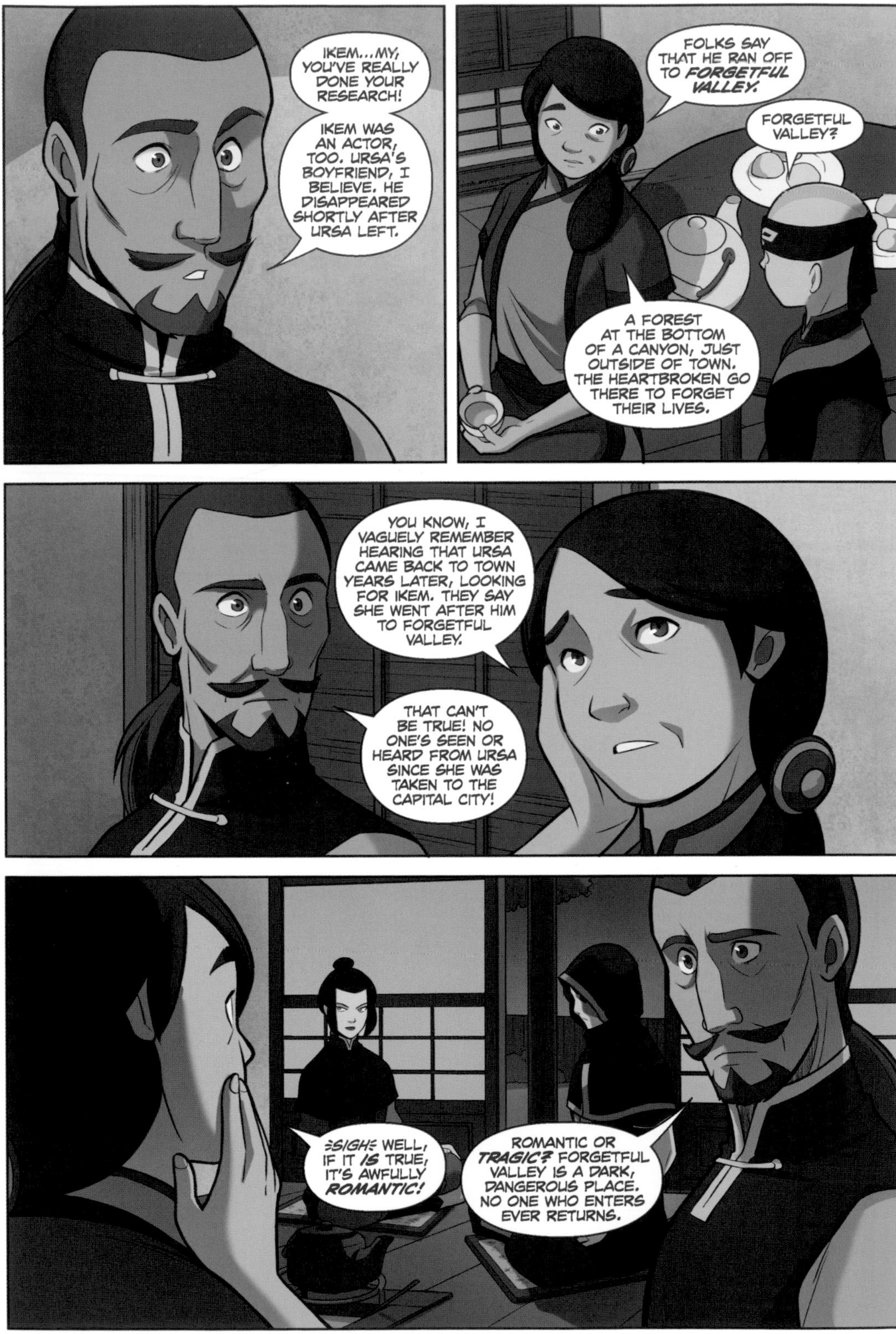

IKEM...MY, YOU'VE REALLY DONE YOUR RESEARCH!
IKEM WAS AN ACTOR, TOO. URSA'S BOYFRIEND, I BELIEVE. HE DISAPPEARED SHORTLY AFTER URSA LEFT.
FOLKS SAY THAT HE RAN OFF TO ***FORGETFUL VALLEY.***
FORGETFUL VALLEY?
A FOREST AT THE BOTTOM OF A CANYON, JUST OUTSIDE OF TOWN. THE HEARTBROKEN GO THERE TO FORGET THEIR LIVES.
YOU KNOW, I VAGUELY REMEMBER HEARING THAT URSA CAME BACK TO TOWN YEARS LATER, LOOKING FOR IKEM. THEY SAY SHE WENT AFTER HIM TO FORGETFUL VALLEY.
THAT CAN'T BE TRUE! NO ONE'S SEEN OR HEARD FROM URSA SINCE SHE WAS TAKEN TO THE CAPITAL CITY!
SIGH WELL, IF IT ***IS*** TRUE, IT'S AWFULLY ***ROMANTIC!***
ROMANTIC OR ***TRAGIC?*** FORGETFUL VALLEY IS A DARK, DANGEROUS PLACE. NO ONE WHO ENTERS EVER RETURNS.

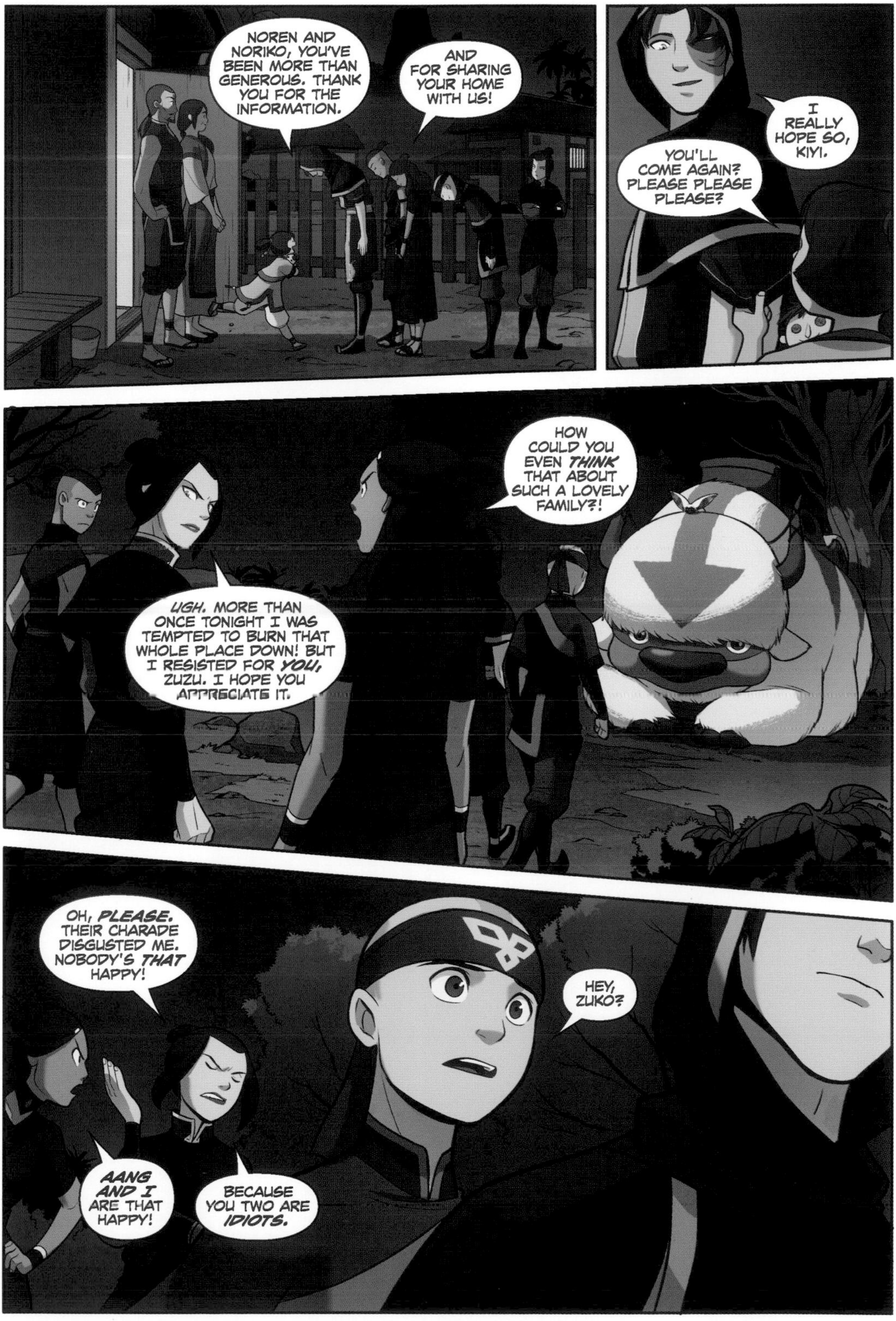
NOREN AND NORIKO, YOU'VE BEEN MORE THAN GENEROUS. THANK YOU FOR THE INFORMATION.
AND FOR SHARING YOUR HOME WITH US!
YOU'LL COME AGAIN? PLEASE PLEASE PLEASE?
I REALLY HOPE SO, KIYI.
UGH. MORE THAN ONCE TONIGHT I WAS TEMPTED TO BURN THAT WHOLE PLACE DOWN! BUT I RESISTED FOR YOU, ZUZU. I HOPE YOU APPRECIATE IT.
HOW COULD YOU EVEN THINK THAT ABOUT SUCH A LOVELY FAMILY?!
OH, PLEASE. THEIR CHARADE DISGUSTED ME. NOBODY'S THAT HAPPY!
AANG AND I ARE THAT HAPPY!
BECAUSE YOU TWO ARE IDIOTS.
HEY, ZUKO?

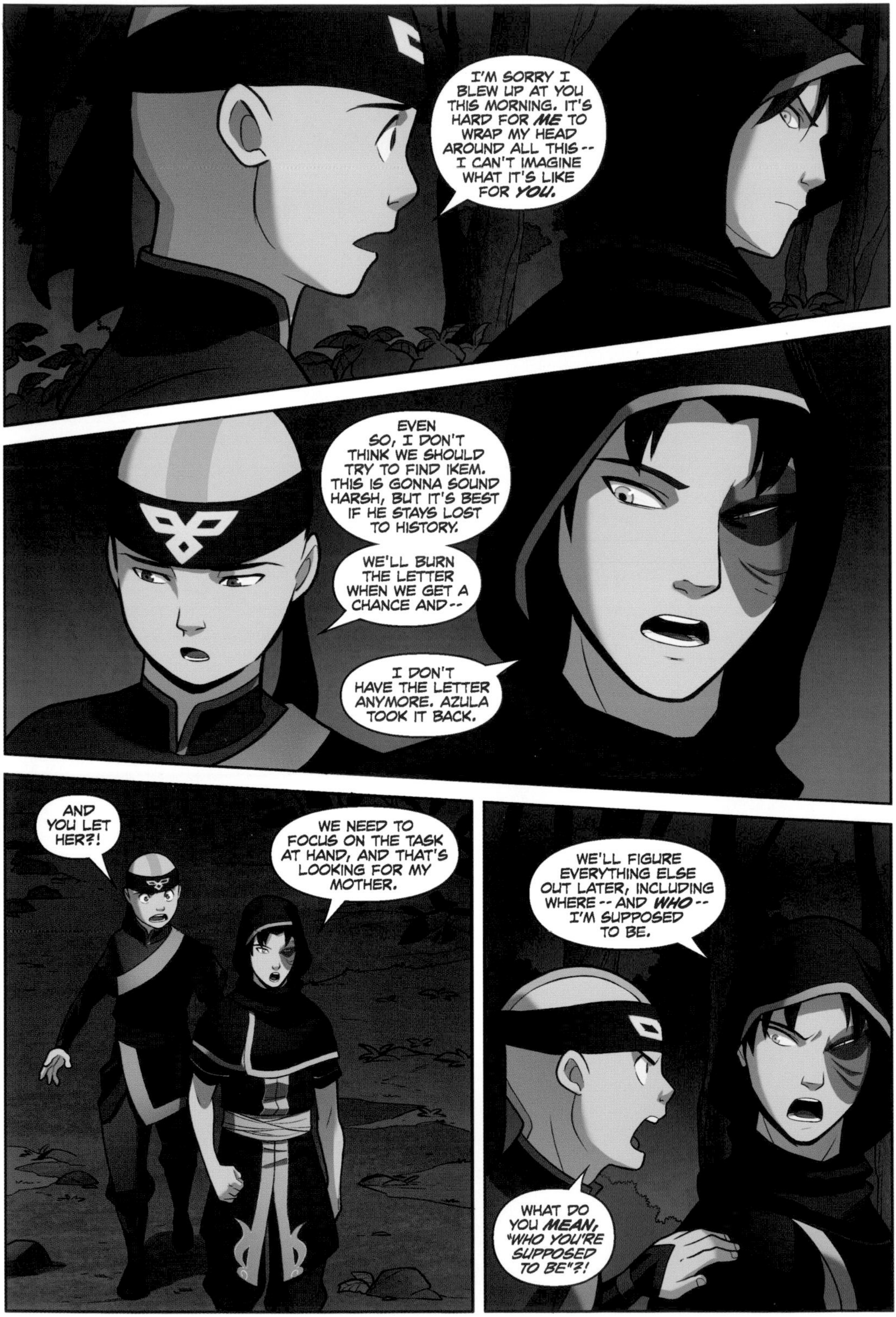
I'M SORRY I BLEW UP AT YOU THIS MORNING. IT'S HARD FOR *ME* TO WRAP MY HEAD AROUND ALL THIS -- I CAN'T IMAGINE WHAT IT'S LIKE FOR *YOU*.
EVEN SO, I DON'T THINK WE SHOULD TRY TO FIND IKEM. THIS IS GONNA SOUND HARSH, BUT IT'S BEST IF HE STAYS LOST TO HISTORY.
WE'LL BURN THE LETTER WHEN WE GET A CHANCE AND --
I DON'T HAVE THE LETTER ANYMORE. AZULA TOOK IT BACK.
AND YOU LET HER?!
WE NEED TO FOCUS ON THE TASK AT HAND, AND THAT'S LOOKING FOR MY MOTHER.
WE'LL FIGURE EVERYTHING ELSE OUT LATER, INCLUDING WHERE -- AND *WHO* -- I'M SUPPOSED TO BE.
WHAT DO YOU *MEAN*, *"WHO YOU'RE SUPPOSED TO BE"*?!

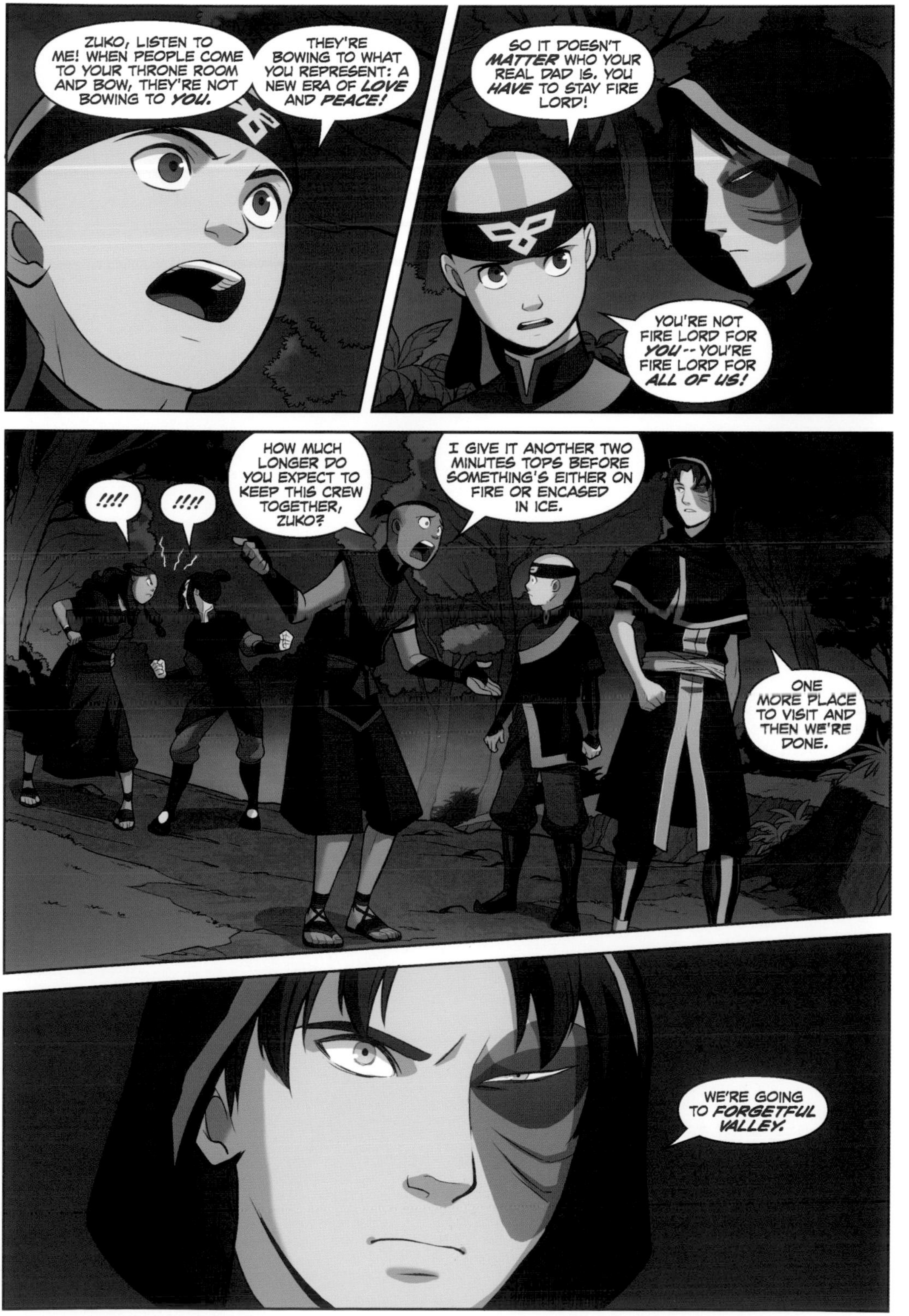
ZUKO, LISTEN TO ME! WHEN PEOPLE COME TO YOUR THRONE ROOM AND BOW, THEY'RE NOT BOWING TO *YOU.*
THEY'RE BOWING TO WHAT YOU REPRESENT: A NEW ERA OF *LOVE* AND *PEACE!*
SO IT DOESN'T *MATTER* WHO YOUR REAL DAD IS. YOU *HAVE* TO STAY FIRE LORD!
YOU'RE NOT FIRE LORD FOR *YOU*-- YOU'RE FIRE LORD FOR *ALL OF US!*
!!!!
!!!!
HOW MUCH LONGER DO YOU EXPECT TO KEEP THIS CREW TOGETHER, ZUKO?
I GIVE IT ANOTHER TWO MINUTES TOPS BEFORE SOMETHING'S EITHER ON FIRE OR ENCASED IN ICE.
ONE MORE PLACE TO VISIT AND THEN WE'RE DONE.
WE'RE GOING TO *FORGETFUL VALLEY.*

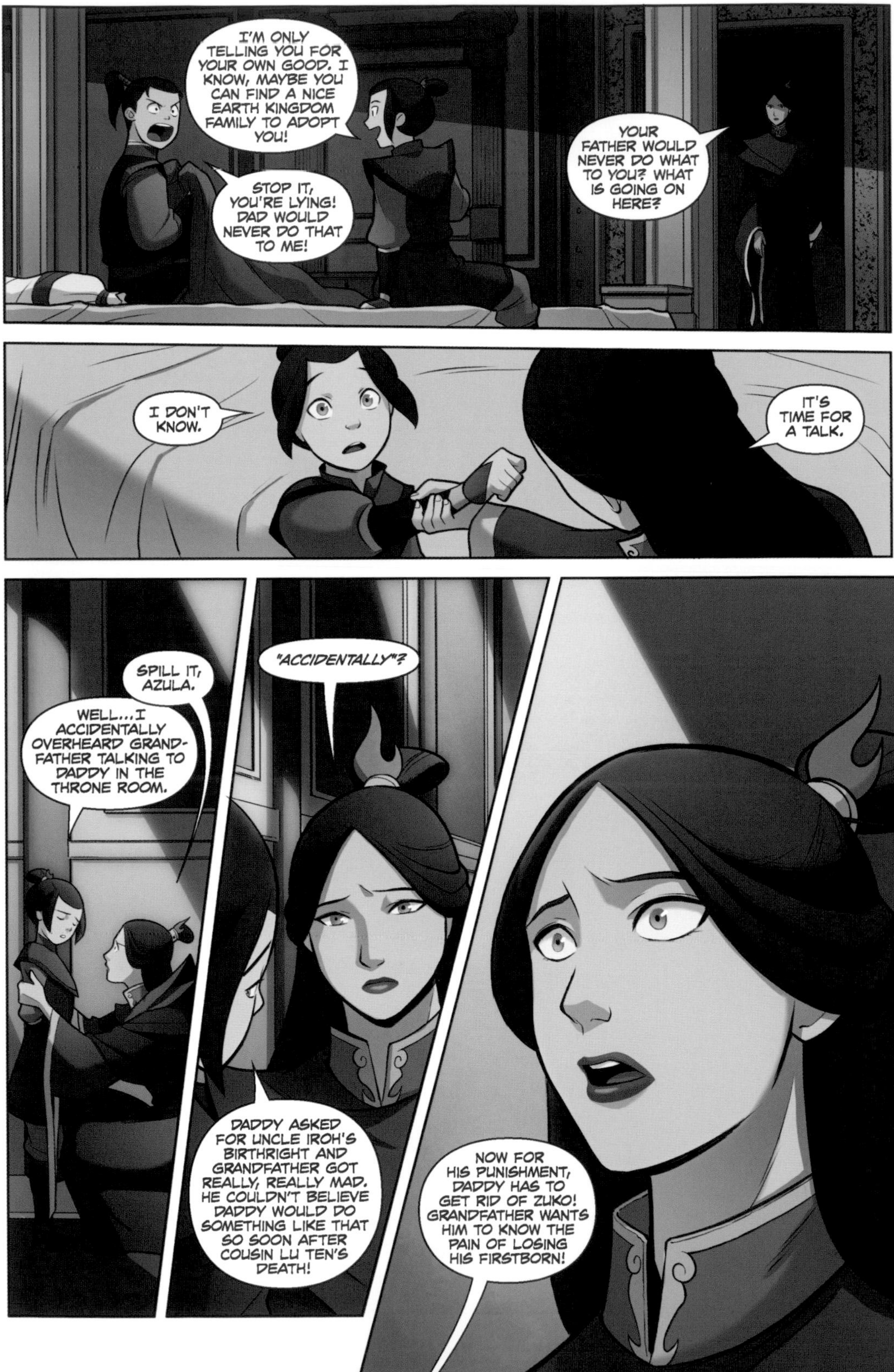
I'M ONLY TELLING YOU FOR YOUR OWN GOOD. I KNOW, MAYBE YOU CAN FIND A NICE EARTH KINGDOM FAMILY TO ADOPT YOU!
STOP IT, YOU'RE LYING! DAD WOULD NEVER DO THAT TO ME!
YOUR FATHER WOULD NEVER DO WHAT TO YOU? WHAT IS GOING ON HERE?
I DON'T KNOW.
IT'S TIME FOR A TALK.
SPILL IT, AZULA.
WELL...I ACCIDENTALLY OVERHEARD GRAND-FATHER TALKING TO DADDY IN THE THRONE ROOM.
"ACCIDENTALLY"?
DADDY ASKED FOR UNCLE IROH'S BIRTHRIGHT AND GRANDFATHER GOT REALLY, REALLY MAD. HE COULDN'T BELIEVE DADDY WOULD DO SOMETHING LIKE THAT SO SOON AFTER COUSIN LU TEN'S DEATH!
NOW FOR HIS PUNISHMENT, DADDY HAS TO GET RID OF ZUKO! GRANDFATHER WANTS HIM TO KNOW THE PAIN OF LOSING HIS FIRSTBORN!

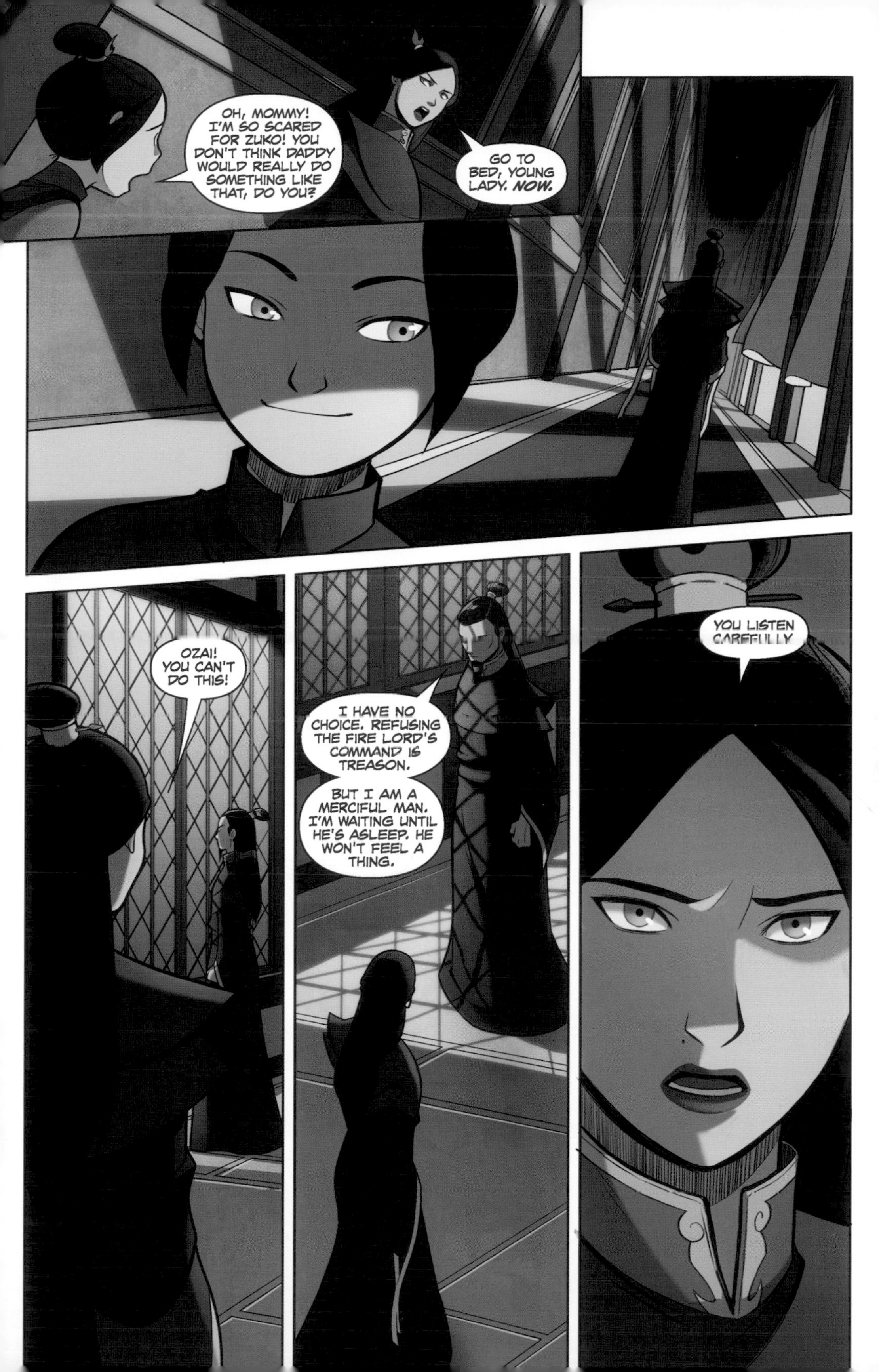
OH, MOMMY! I'M SO SCARED FOR ZUKO! YOU DON'T THINK DADDY WOULD REALLY DO SOMETHING LIKE THAT, DO YOU?
GO TO BED, YOUNG LADY. ***NOW.***
OZAI! YOU CAN'T DO THIS!
I HAVE NO CHOICE. REFUSING THE FIRE LORD'S COMMAND IS TREASON.
BUT I AM A MERCIFUL MAN. I'M WAITING UNTIL HE'S ASLEEP. HE WON'T FEEL A THING.
YOU LISTEN CAREFULLY

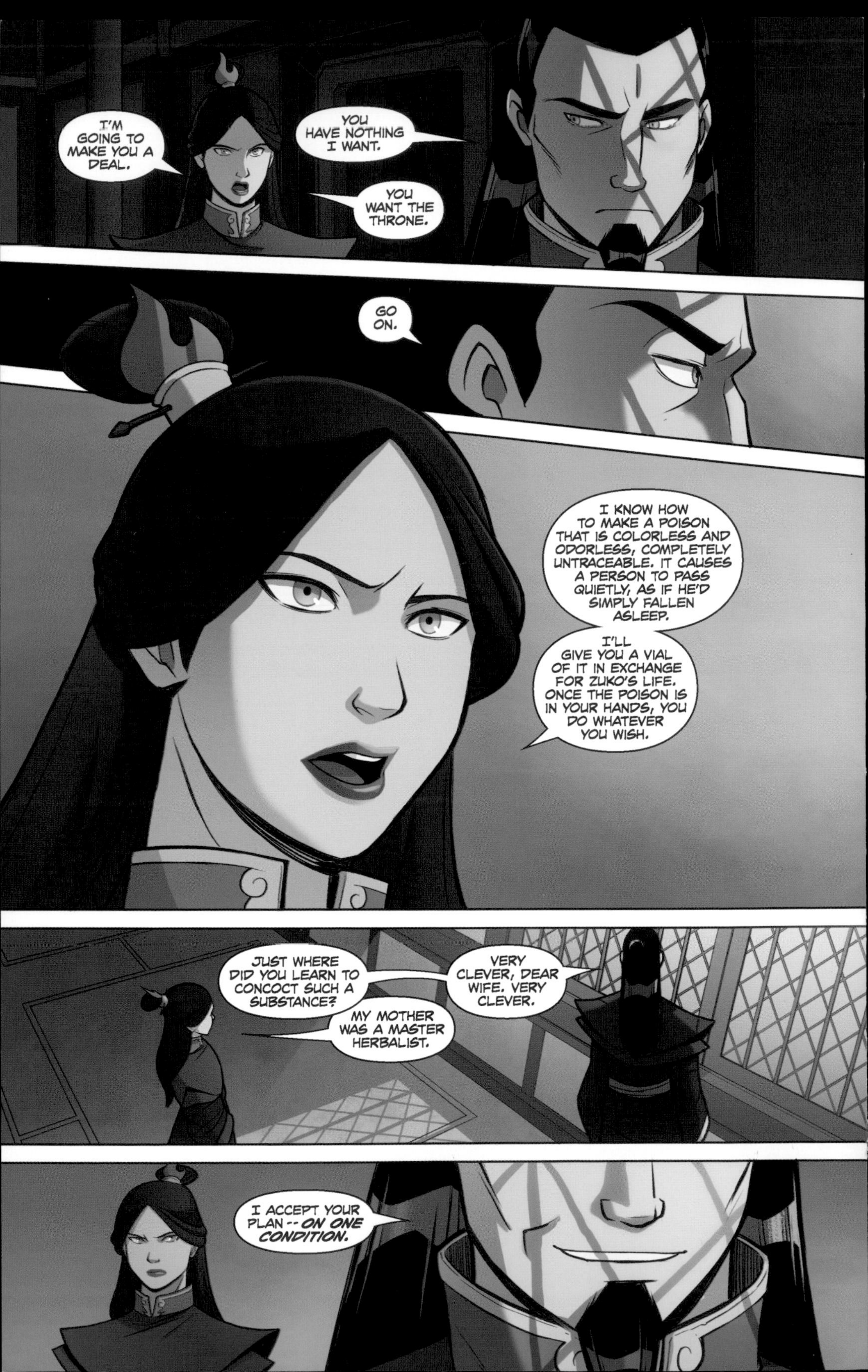
I'M GOING TO MAKE YOU A DEAL.
YOU HAVE NOTHING I WANT.
YOU WANT THE THRONE.
GO ON.
I KNOW HOW TO MAKE A POISON THAT IS COLORLESS AND ODORLESS, COMPLETELY UNTRACEABLE. IT CAUSES A PERSON TO PASS QUIETLY, AS IF HE'D SIMPLY FALLEN ASLEEP.
I'LL GIVE YOU A VIAL OF IT IN EXCHANGE FOR ZUKO'S LIFE. ONCE THE POISON IS IN YOUR HANDS, YOU DO WHATEVER YOU WISH.
VERY CLEVER, DEAR WIFE. VERY CLEVER.
JUST WHERE DID YOU LEARN TO CONCOCT SUCH A SUBSTANCE?
MY MOTHER WAS A MASTER HERBALIST.
I ACCEPT YOUR PLAN -- *ON ONE CONDITION.*

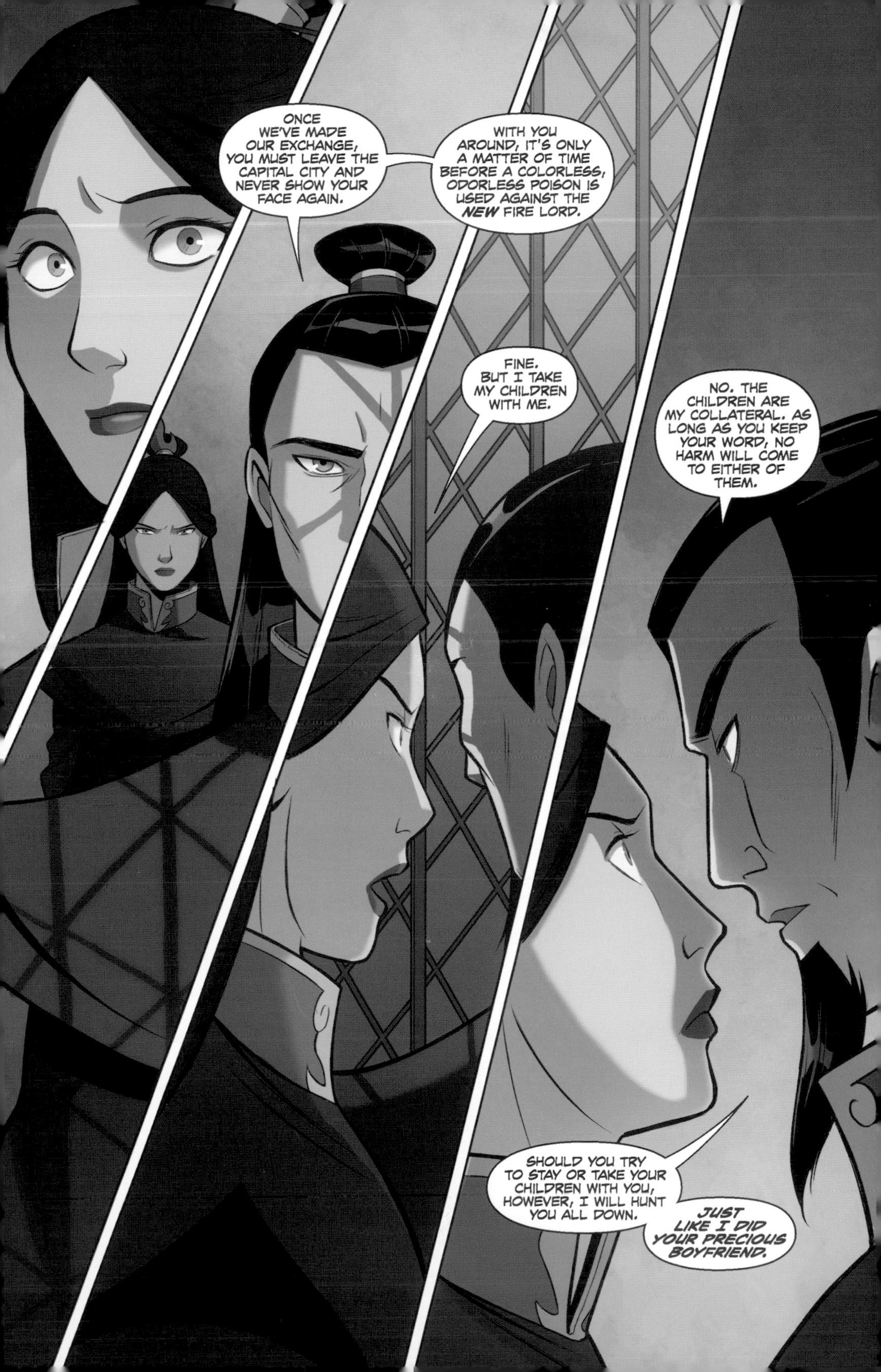
ONCE WE'VE MADE OUR EXCHANGE, YOU MUST LEAVE THE CAPITAL CITY AND NEVER SHOW YOUR FACE AGAIN.
WITH YOU AROUND, IT'S ONLY A MATTER OF TIME BEFORE A COLORLESS, ODORLESS POISON IS USED AGAINST THE *NEW* FIRE LORD.
FINE. BUT I TAKE MY CHILDREN WITH ME.
NO. THE CHILDREN ARE MY COLLATERAL. AS LONG AS YOU KEEP YOUR WORD, NO HARM WILL COME TO EITHER OF THEM.
SHOULD YOU TRY TO STAY OR TAKE YOUR CHILDREN WITH YOU, HOWEVER, I WILL HUNT YOU ALL DOWN.
JUST LIKE I DID YOUR PRECIOUS BOYFRIEND.

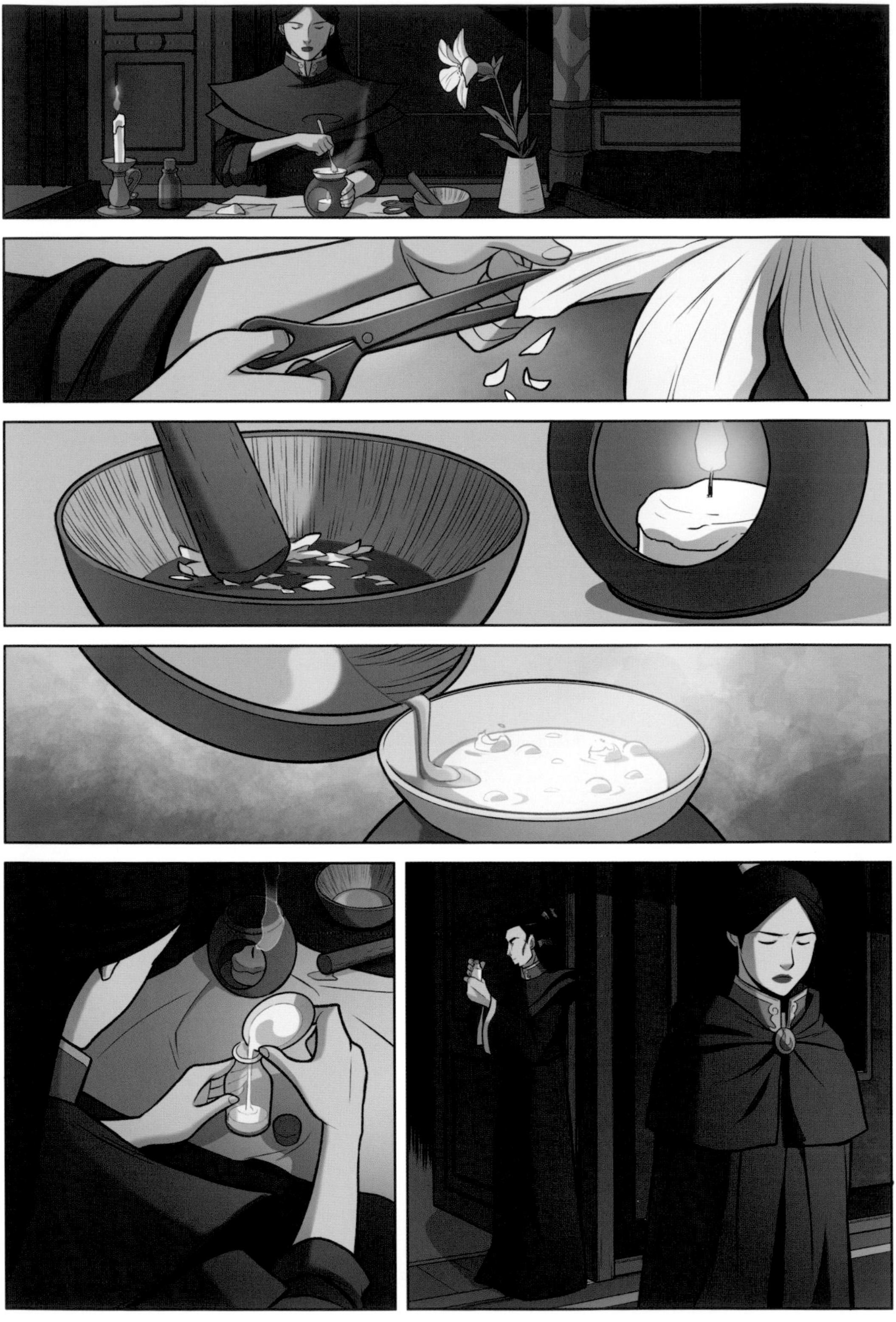

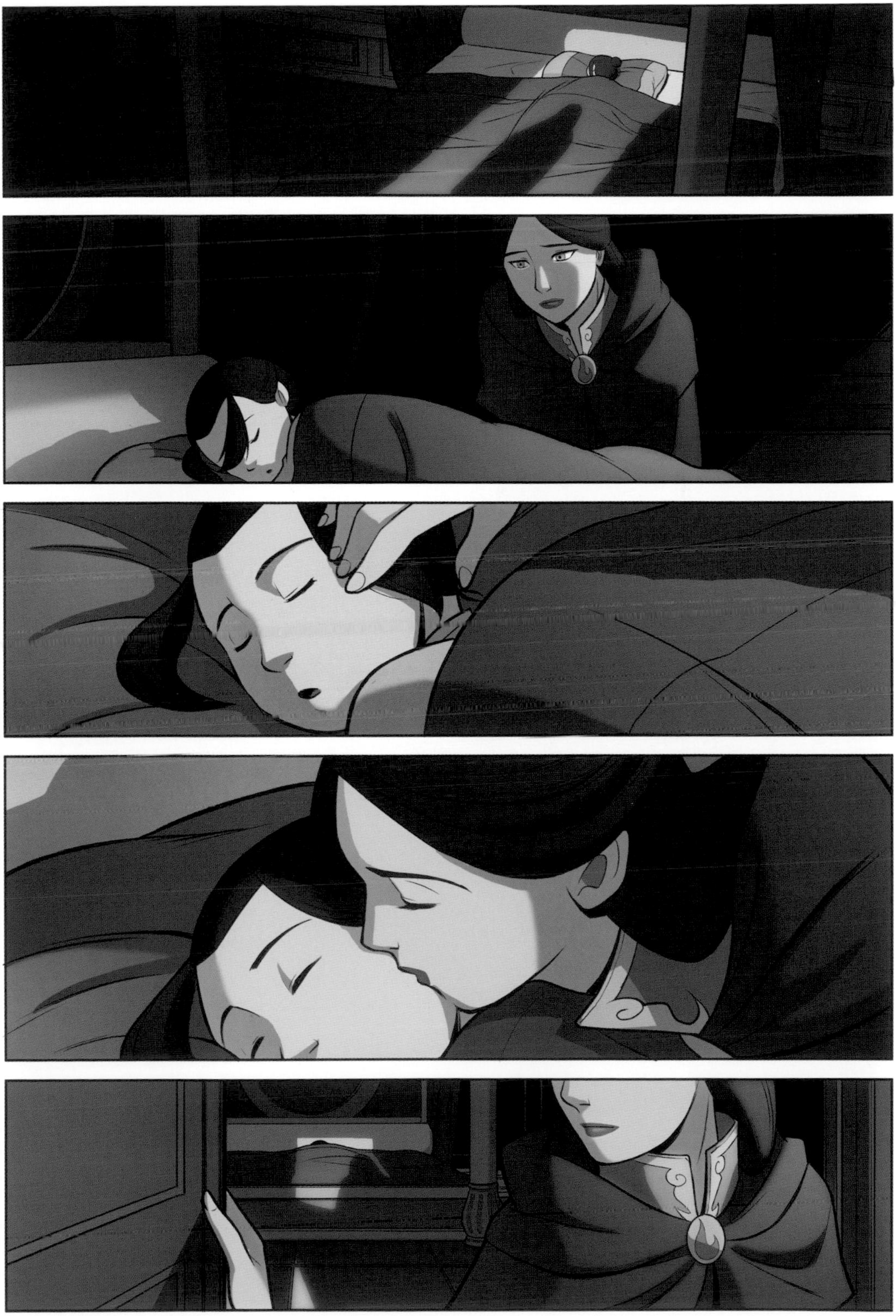

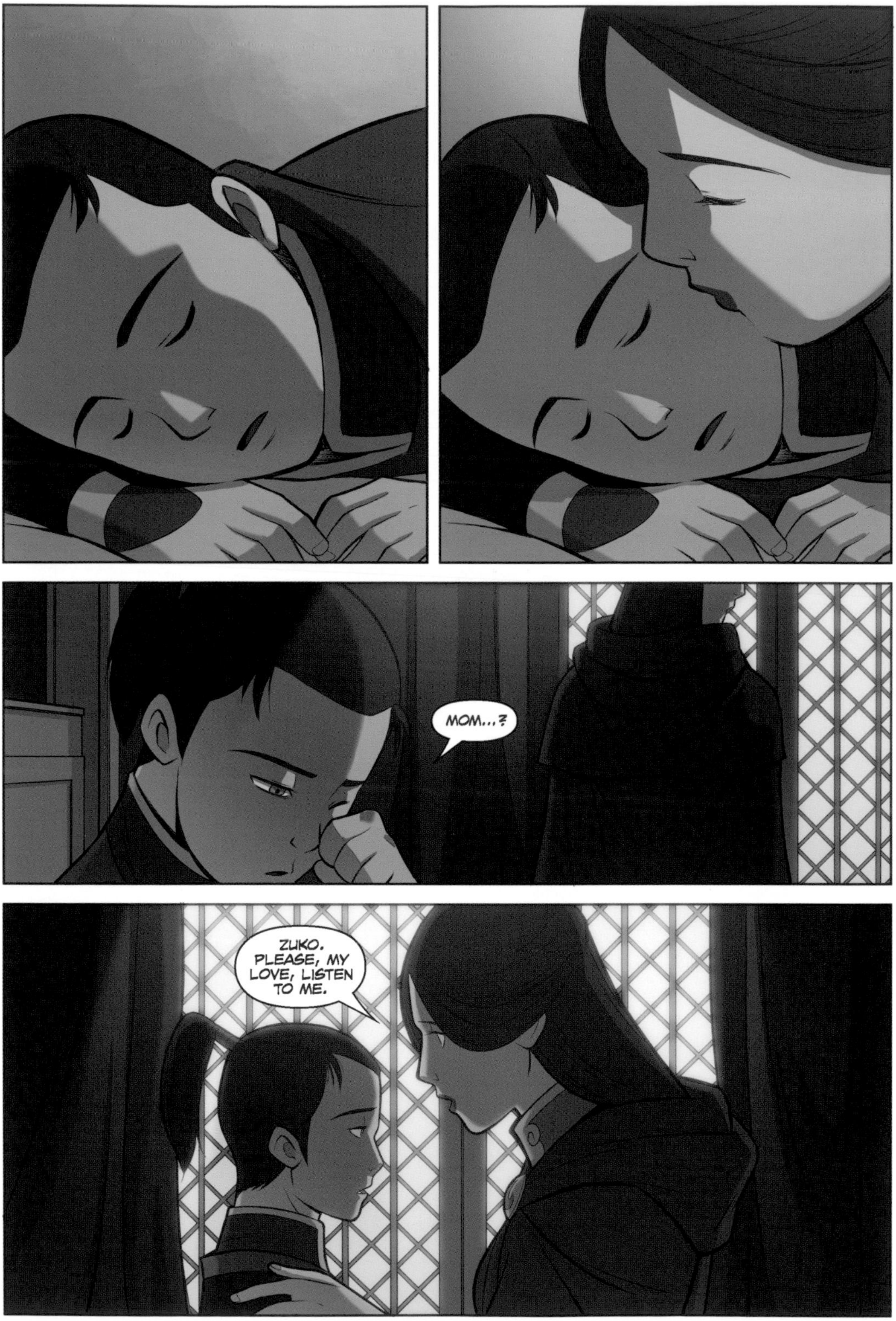
MOM...?
ZUKO. PLEASE, MY LOVE, LISTEN TO ME.

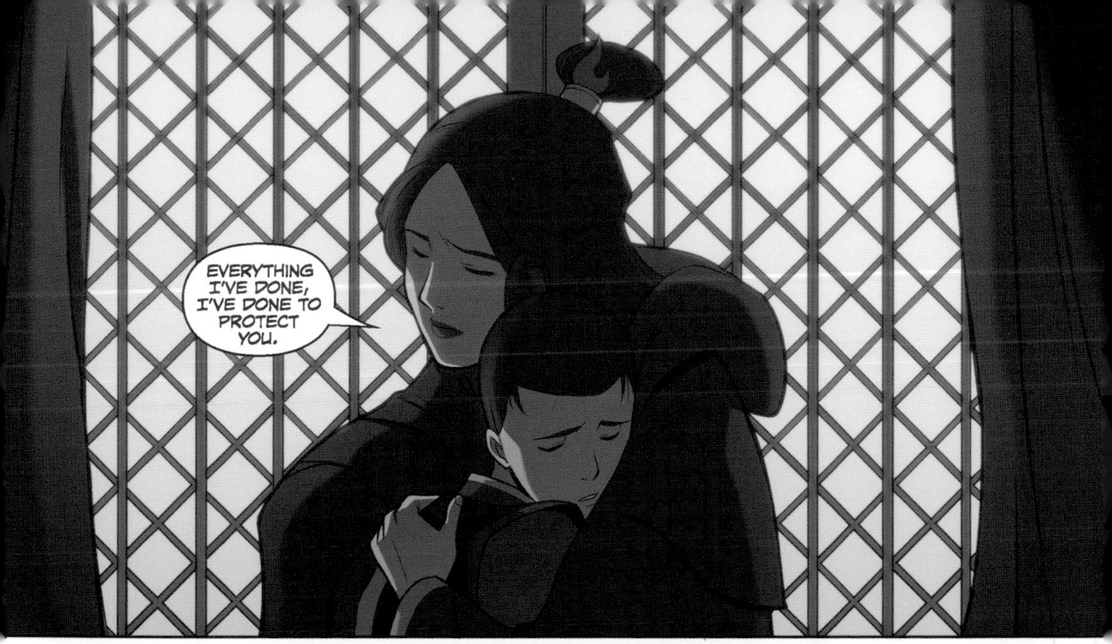
EVERYTHING I'VE DONE, I'VE DONE TO PROTECT YOU.

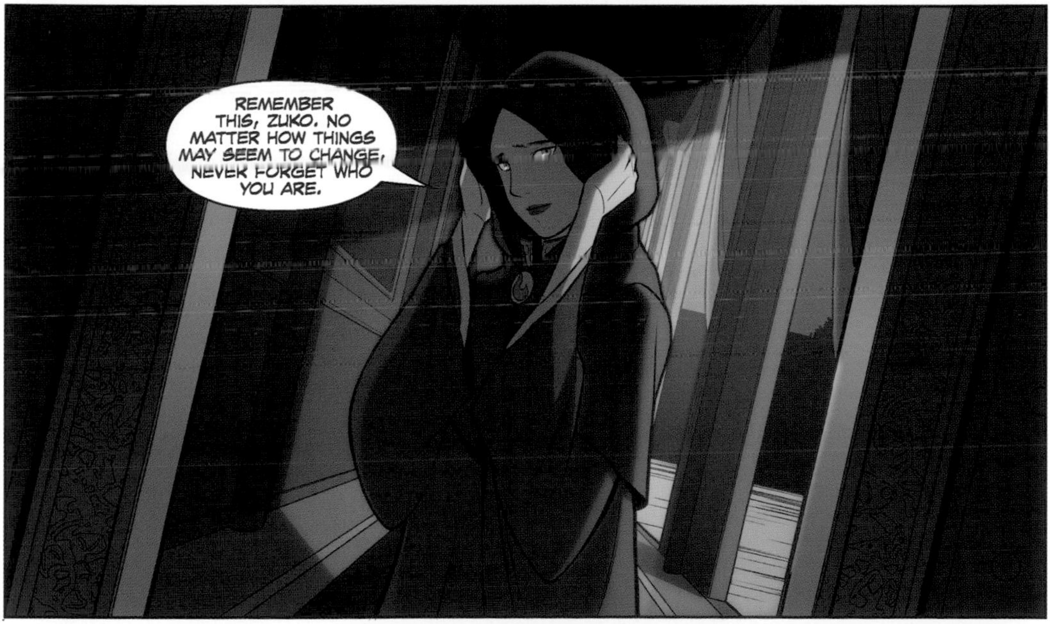
REMEMBER THIS, ZUKO. NO MATTER HOW THINGS MAY SEEM TO CHANGE, NEVER FORGET WHO YOU ARE.

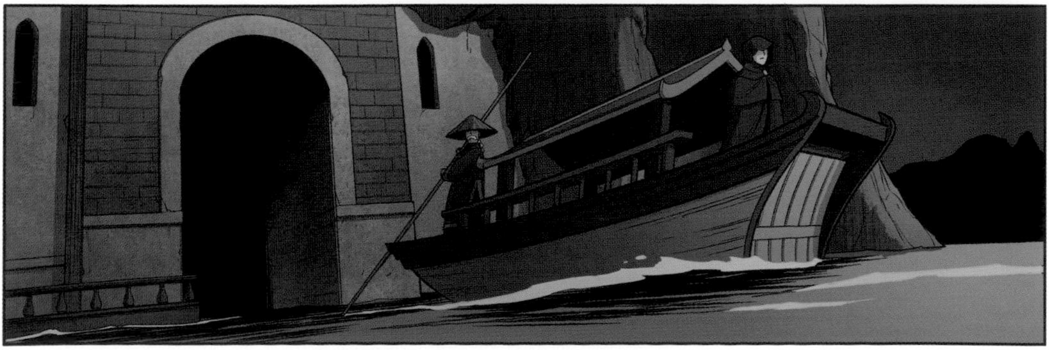

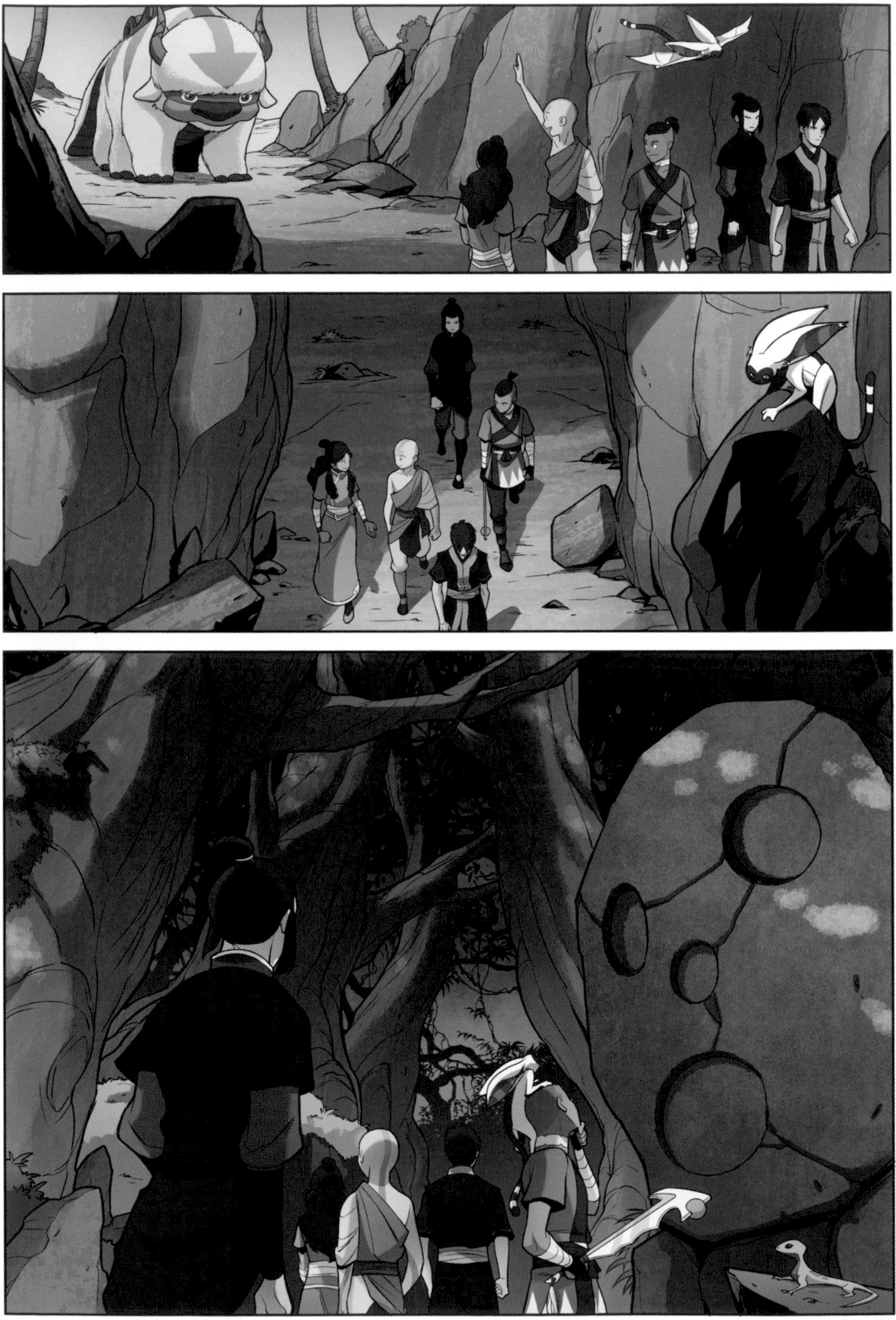

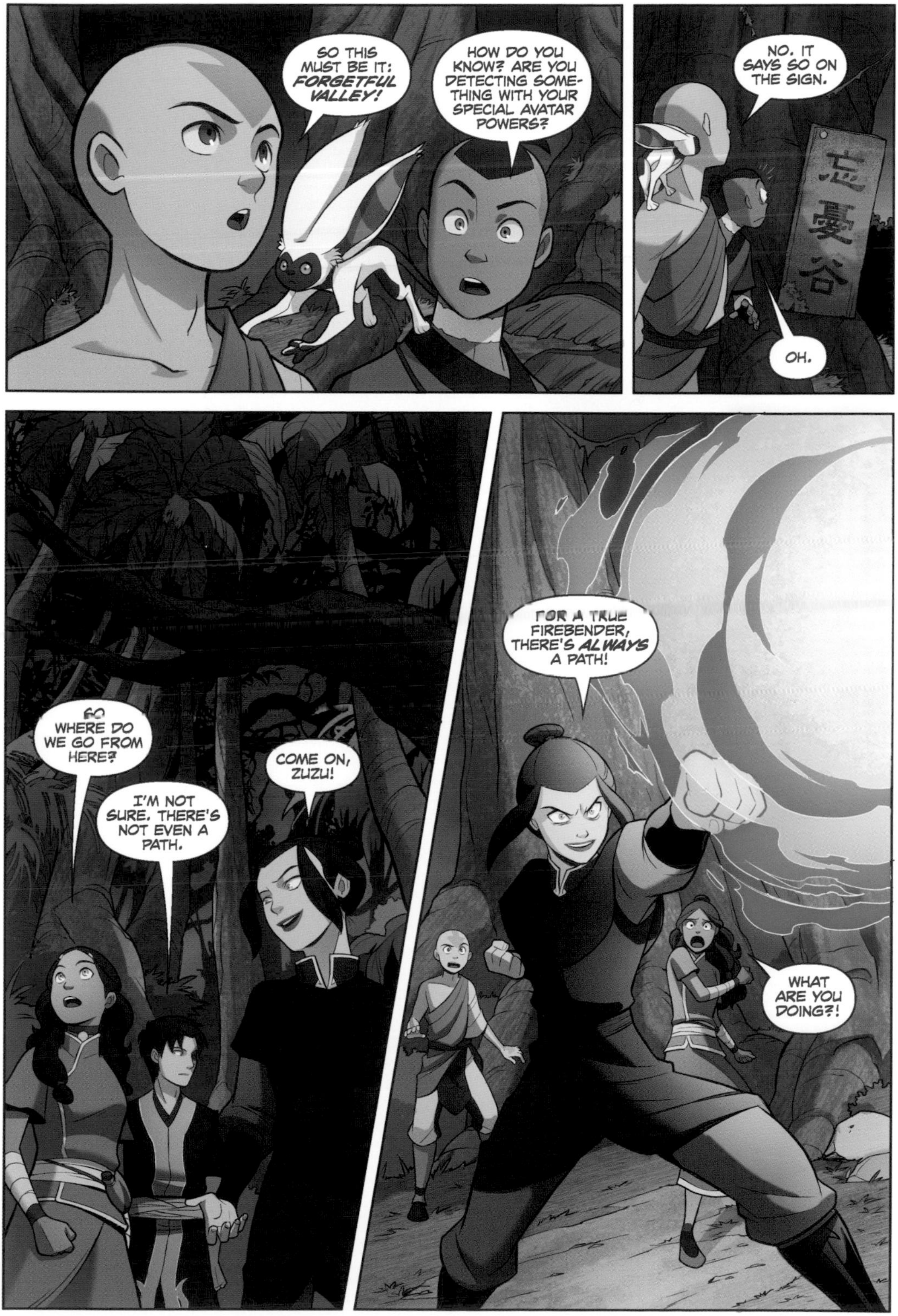
SO THIS MUST BE IT: *FORGETFUL VALLEY!*
HOW DO YOU KNOW? ARE YOU DETECTING SOME-THING WITH YOUR SPECIAL AVATAR POWERS?
NO. IT SAYS SO ON THE SIGN.
忘憂谷
OH.
SO WHERE DO WE GO FROM HERE?
I'M NOT SURE. THERE'S NOT EVEN A PATH.
COME ON, ZUZU!
FOR A TRUE FIREBENDER, THERE'S *ALWAYS* A PATH!
WHAT ARE YOU DOING?!

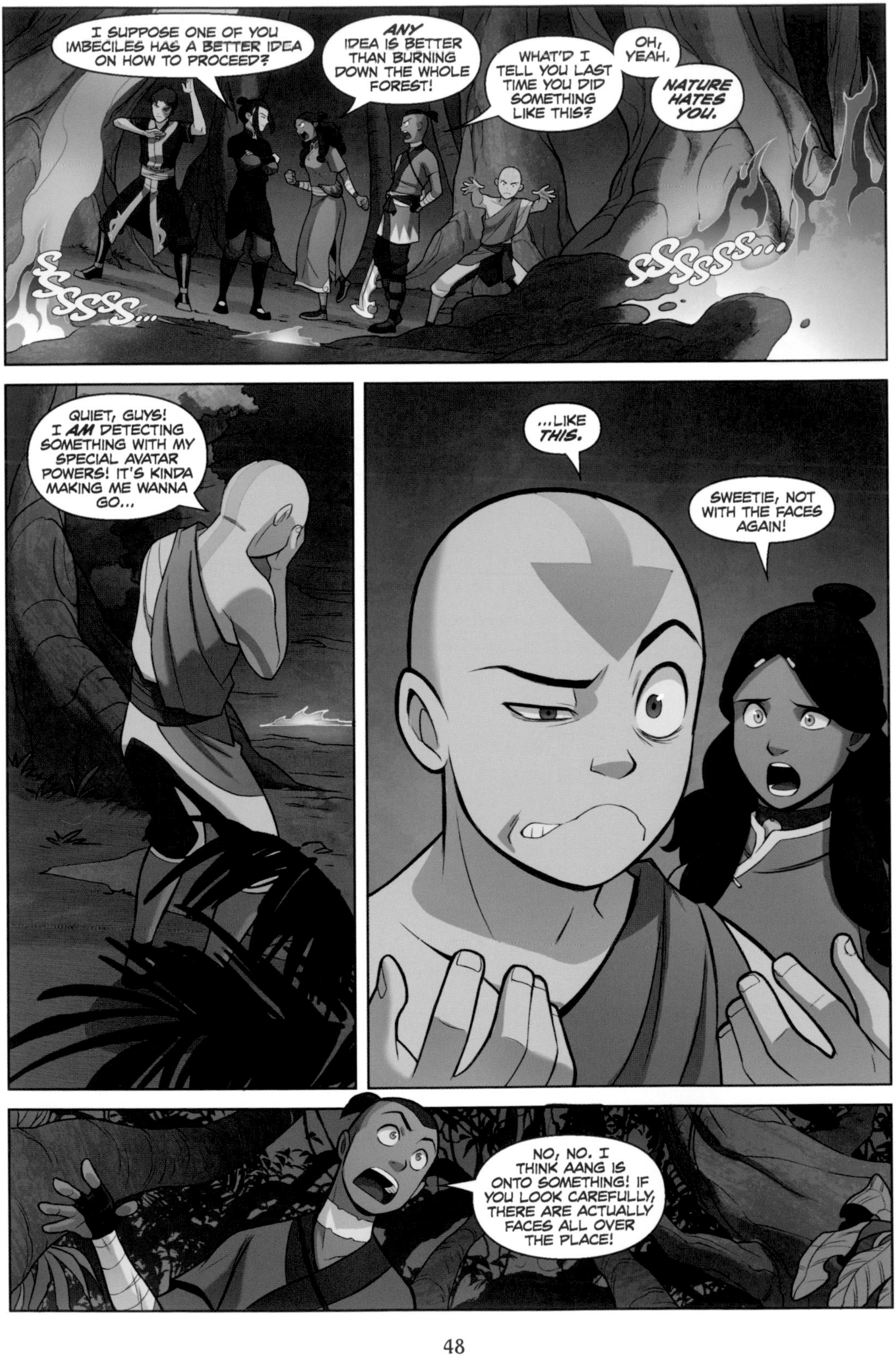
I SUPPOSE ONE OF YOU IMBECILES HAS A BETTER IDEA ON HOW TO PROCEED?
ANY IDEA IS BETTER THAN BURNING DOWN THE WHOLE FOREST!
WHAT'D I TELL YOU LAST TIME YOU DID SOMETHING LIKE THIS?
OH, YEAH.
NATURE HATES YOU.
SSSSSS...
SSSSSS...
QUIET, GUYS! I AM DETECTING SOMETHING WITH MY SPECIAL AVATAR POWERS! IT'S KINDA MAKING ME WANNA GO...
...LIKE THIS.
SWEETIE, NOT WITH THE FACES AGAIN!
NO, NO. I THINK AANG IS ONTO SOMETHING! IF YOU LOOK CAREFULLY, THERE ARE ACTUALLY FACES ALL OVER THE PLACE!

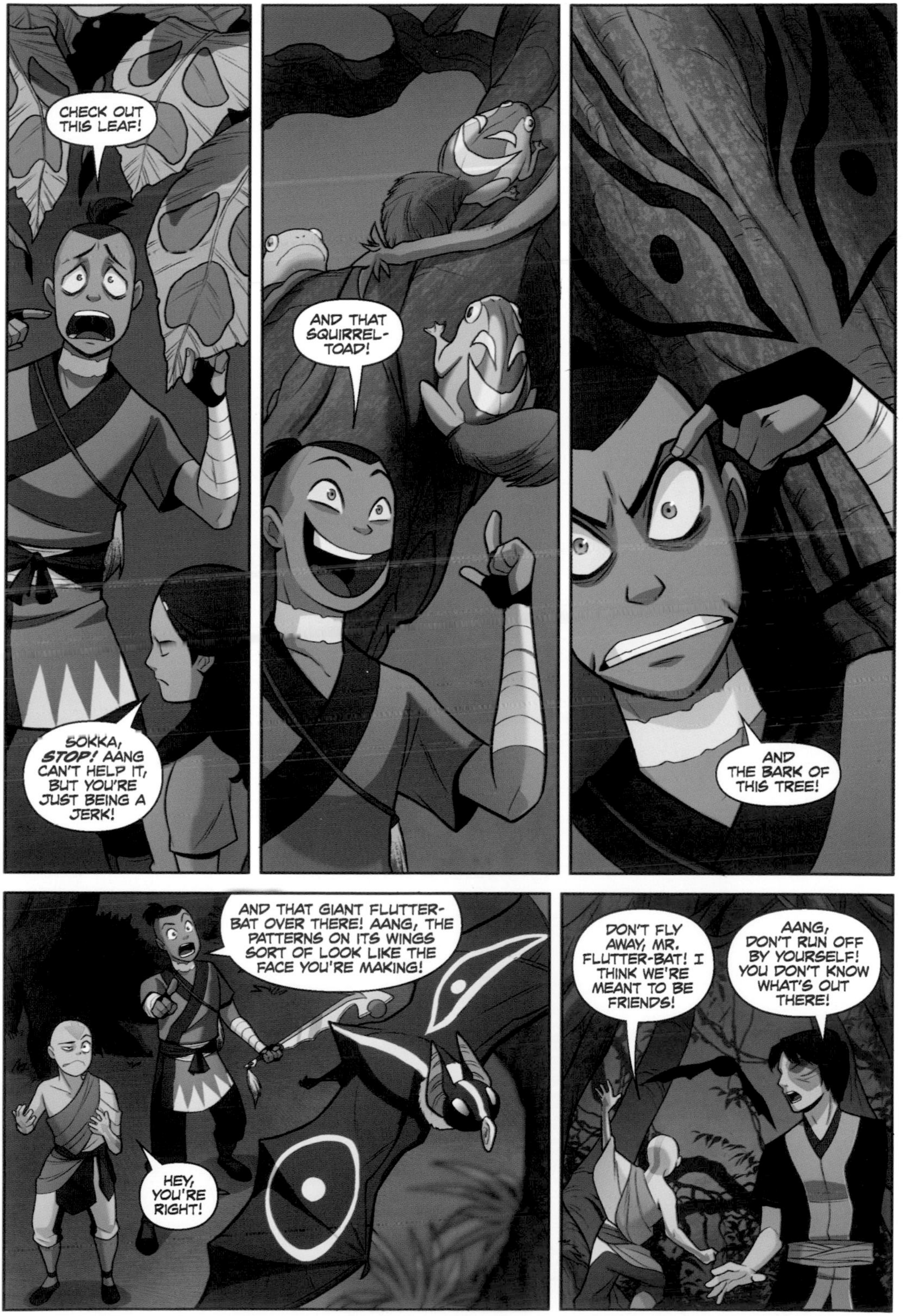

CHECK OUT THIS LEAF!
SOKKA, STOP! AANG CAN'T HELP IT, BUT YOU'RE JUST BEING A JERK!
AND THAT SQUIRREL-TOAD!
AND THE BARK OF THIS TREE!
AND THAT GIANT FLUTTER-BAT OVER THERE! AANG, THE PATTERNS ON ITS WINGS SORT OF LOOK LIKE THE FACE YOU'RE MAKING!
HEY, YOU'RE RIGHT!
DON'T FLY AWAY, MR. FLUTTER-BAT! I THINK WE'RE MEANT TO BE FRIENDS!
AANG, DON'T RUN OFF BY YOURSELF! YOU DON'T KNOW WHAT'S OUT THERE!

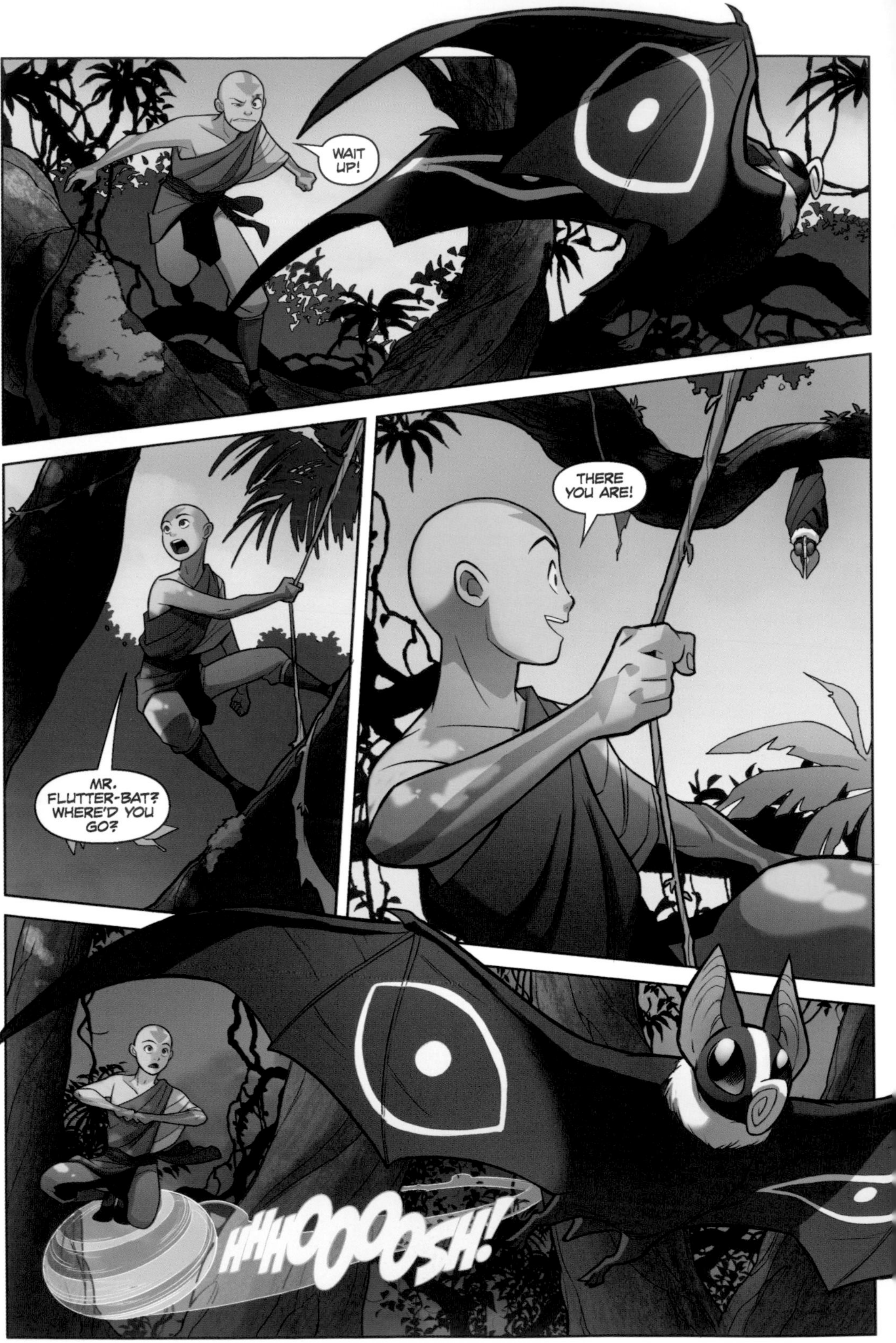
WAIT UP!
MR. FLUTTER-BAT? WHERE'D YOU GO?
THERE YOU ARE!
HHHOOOOOSH!

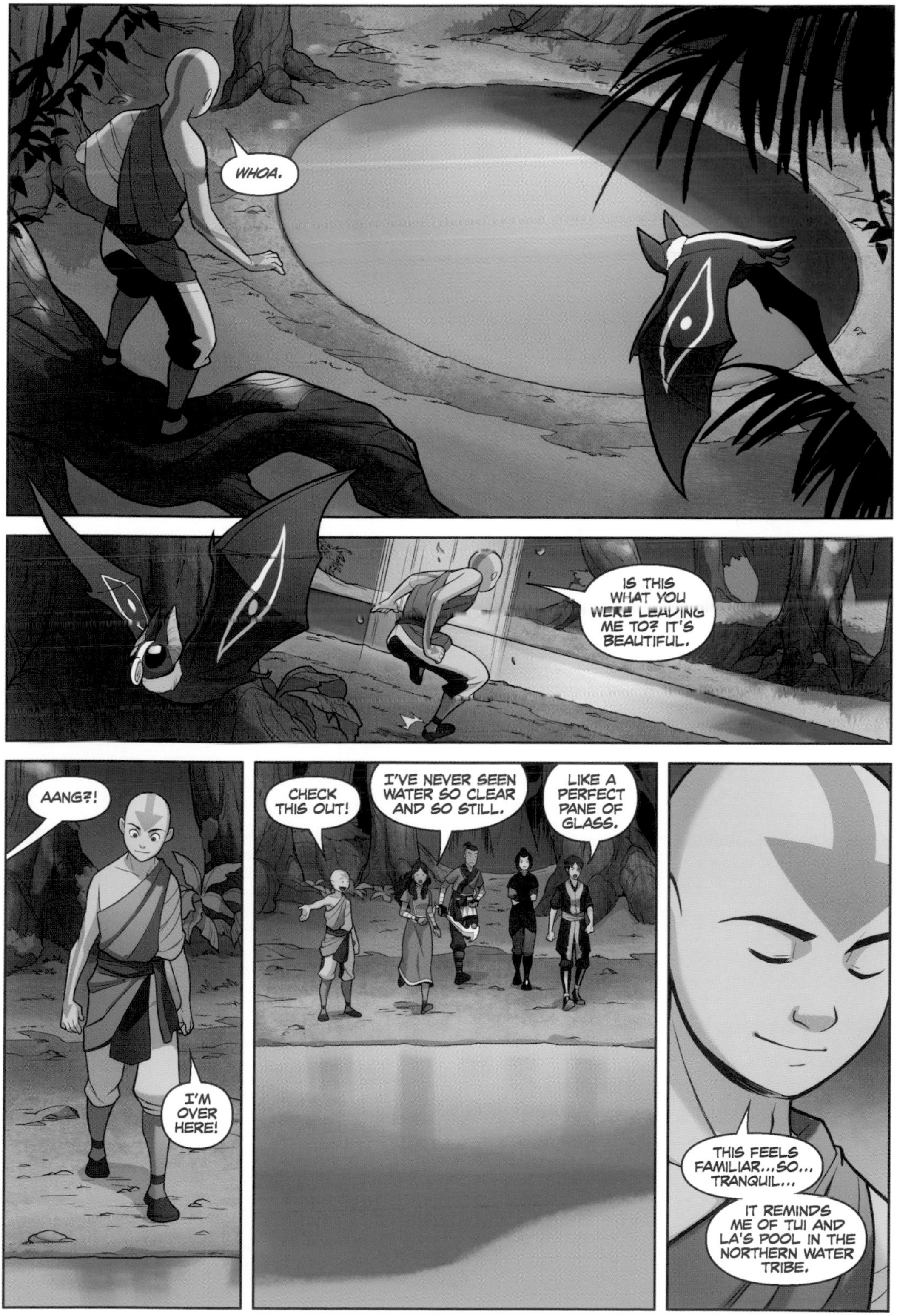
WHOA.
IS THIS WHAT YOU WERE LEADING ME TO? IT'S BEAUTIFUL.
AANG?!
I'M OVER HERE!
CHECK THIS OUT!
I'VE NEVER SEEN WATER SO CLEAR AND SO STILL.
LIKE A PERFECT PANE OF GLASS.
THIS FEELS FAMILIAR...SO... TRANQUIL...
IT REMINDS ME OF TUI AND LA'S POOL IN THE NORTHERN WATER TRIBE.

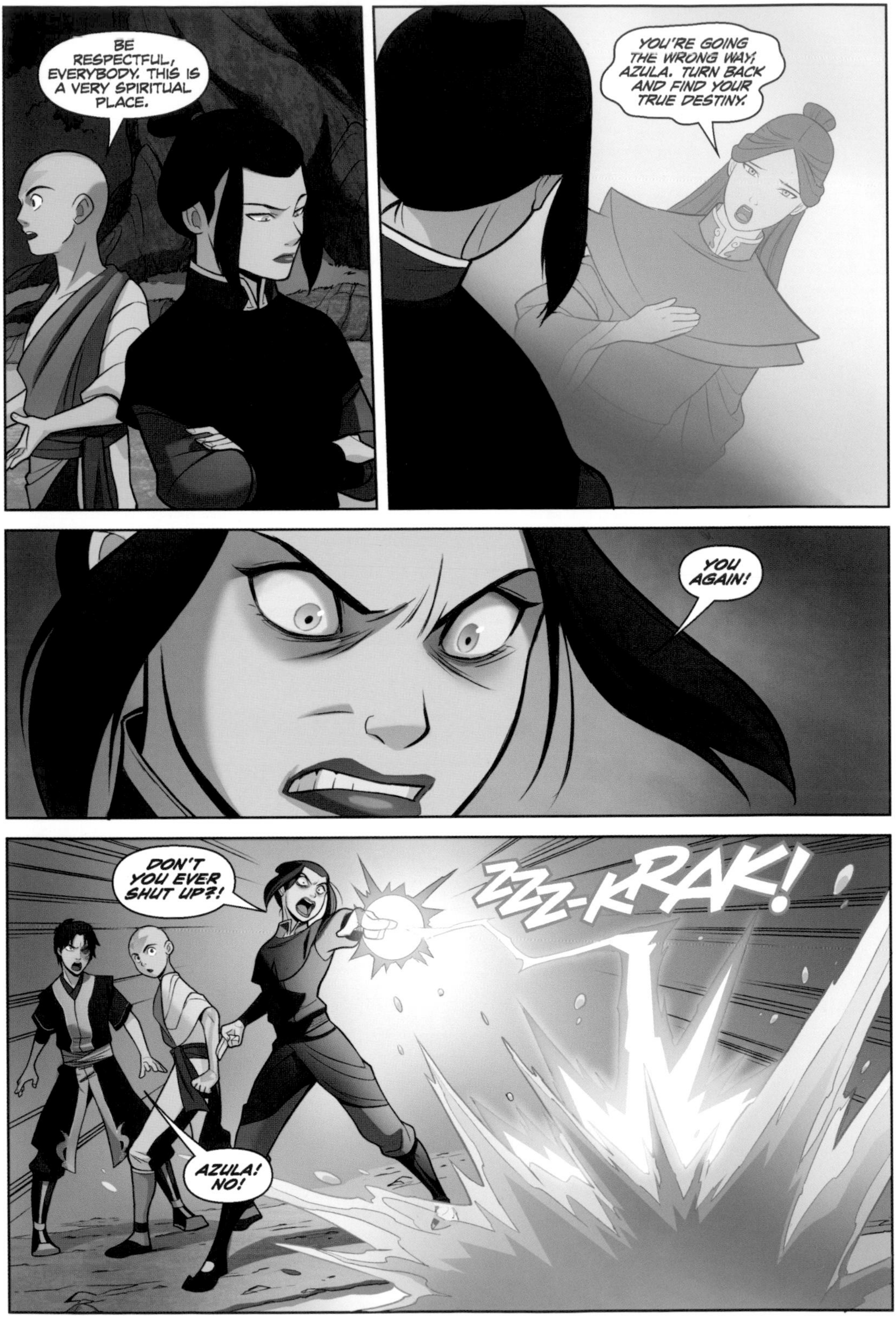

BE RESPECTFUL, EVERYBODY. THIS IS A VERY SPIRITUAL PLACE.
YOU'RE GOING THE WRONG WAY, AZULA. TURN BACK AND FIND YOUR TRUE DESTINY.
YOU AGAIN!
DON'T YOU EVER SHUT UP?!
ZZZ-KRAK!
AZULA! NO!

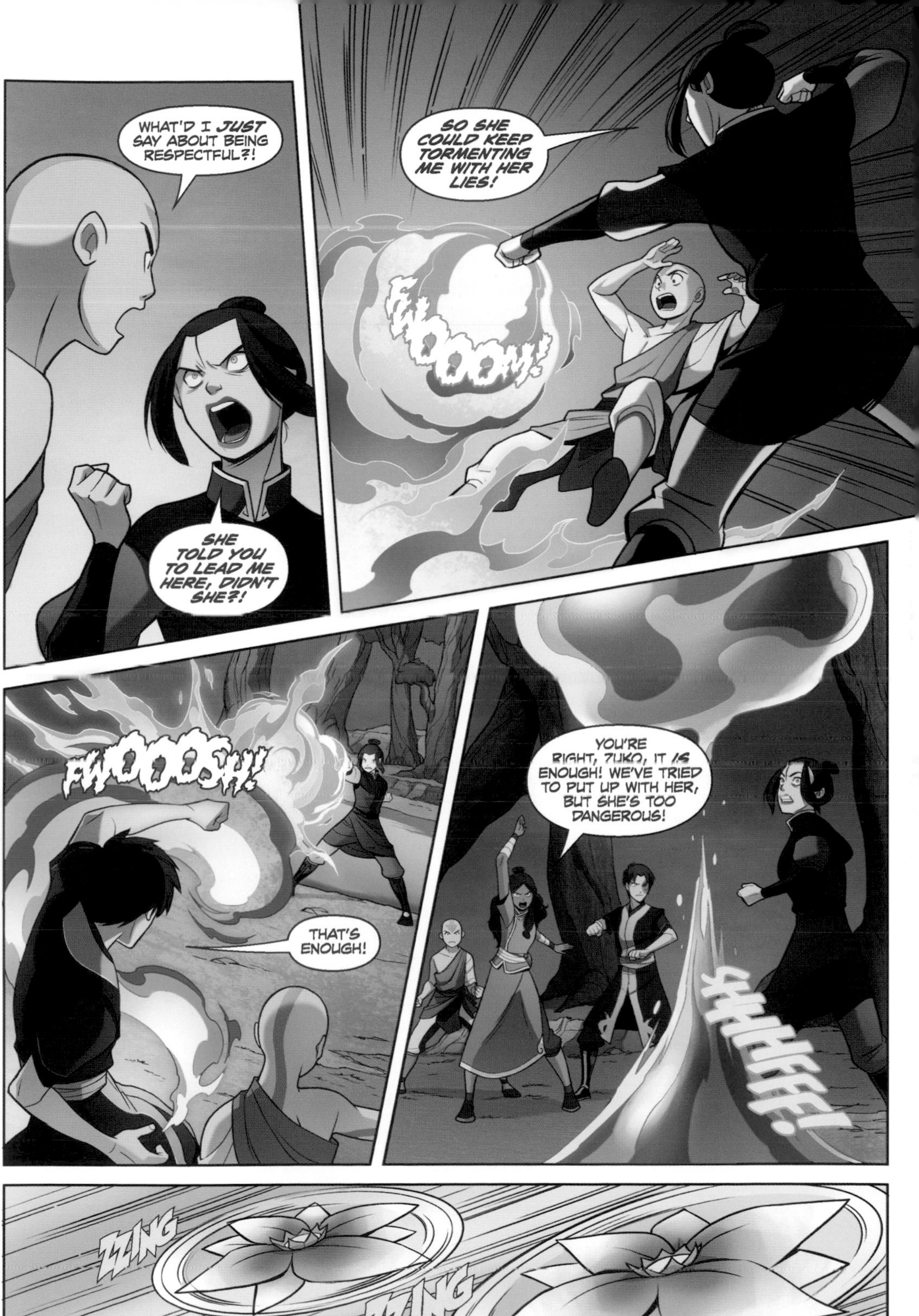
WHAT'D I JUST SAY ABOUT BEING RESPECTFUL?!
SHE TOLD YOU TO LEAD ME HERE, DIDN'T SHE?!
SO SHE COULD KEEP TORMENTING ME WITH HER LIES!
FWOOOM!
FWOOOSH!
THAT'S ENOUGH!
YOU'RE RIGHT, ZUKO, IT IS ENOUGH! WE'VE TRIED TO PUT UP WITH HER, BUT SHE'S TOO DANGEROUS!
SHHHFFF!
ZZING
ZZING

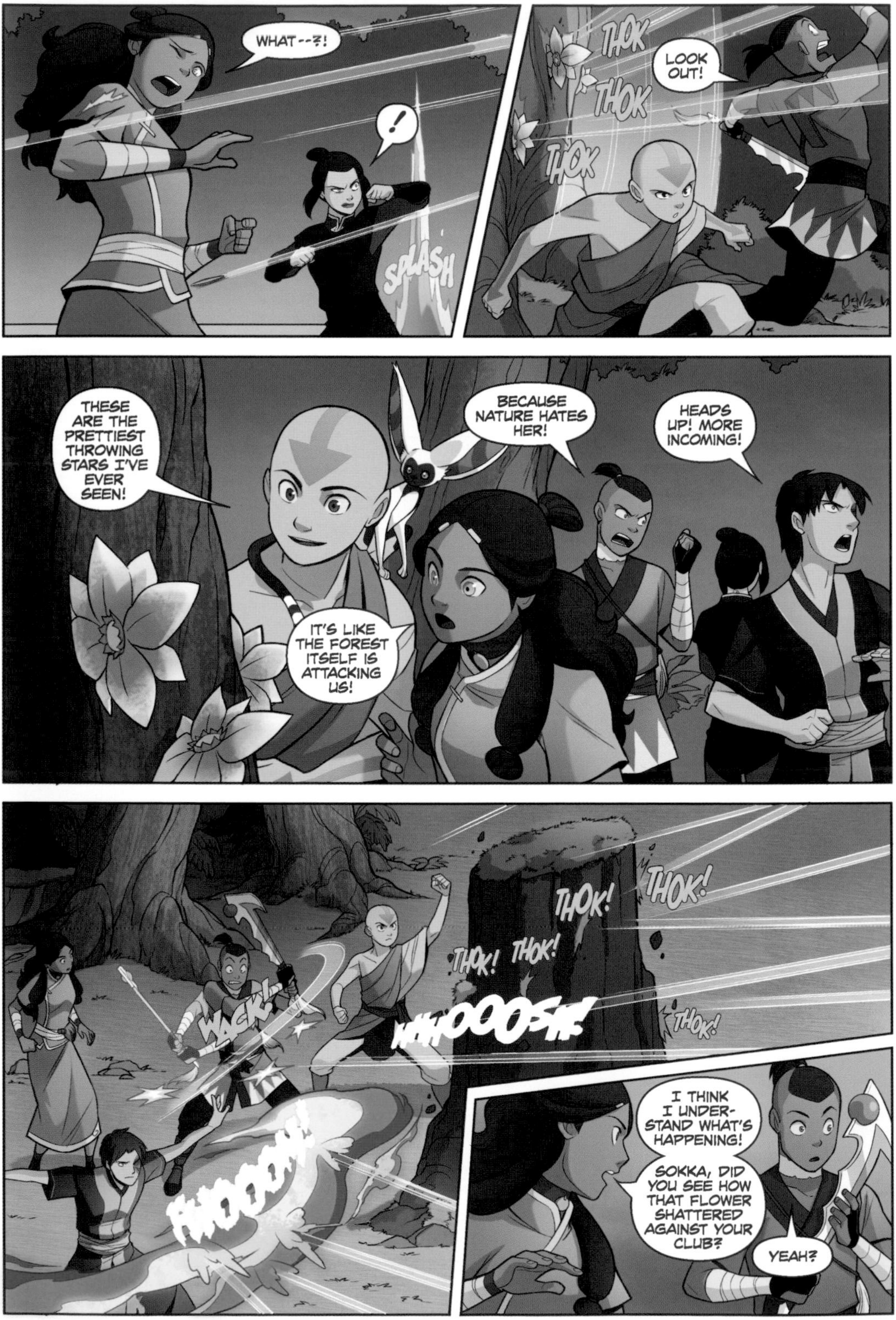
WHAT--?!
!
SPLASH
THOK
LOOK OUT!
THOK
THOK
THESE ARE THE PRETTIEST THROWING STARS I'VE EVER SEEN!
BECAUSE NATURE HATES HER!
HEADS UP! MORE INCOMING!
IT'S LIKE THE FOREST ITSELF IS ATTACKING US!
THOK!
THOK!
THOK!
THOK!
WACK!
THOK!
I THINK I UNDER-STAND WHAT'S HAPPENING!
SOKKA, DID YOU SEE HOW THAT FLOWER SHATTERED AGAINST YOUR CLUB?
YEAH?

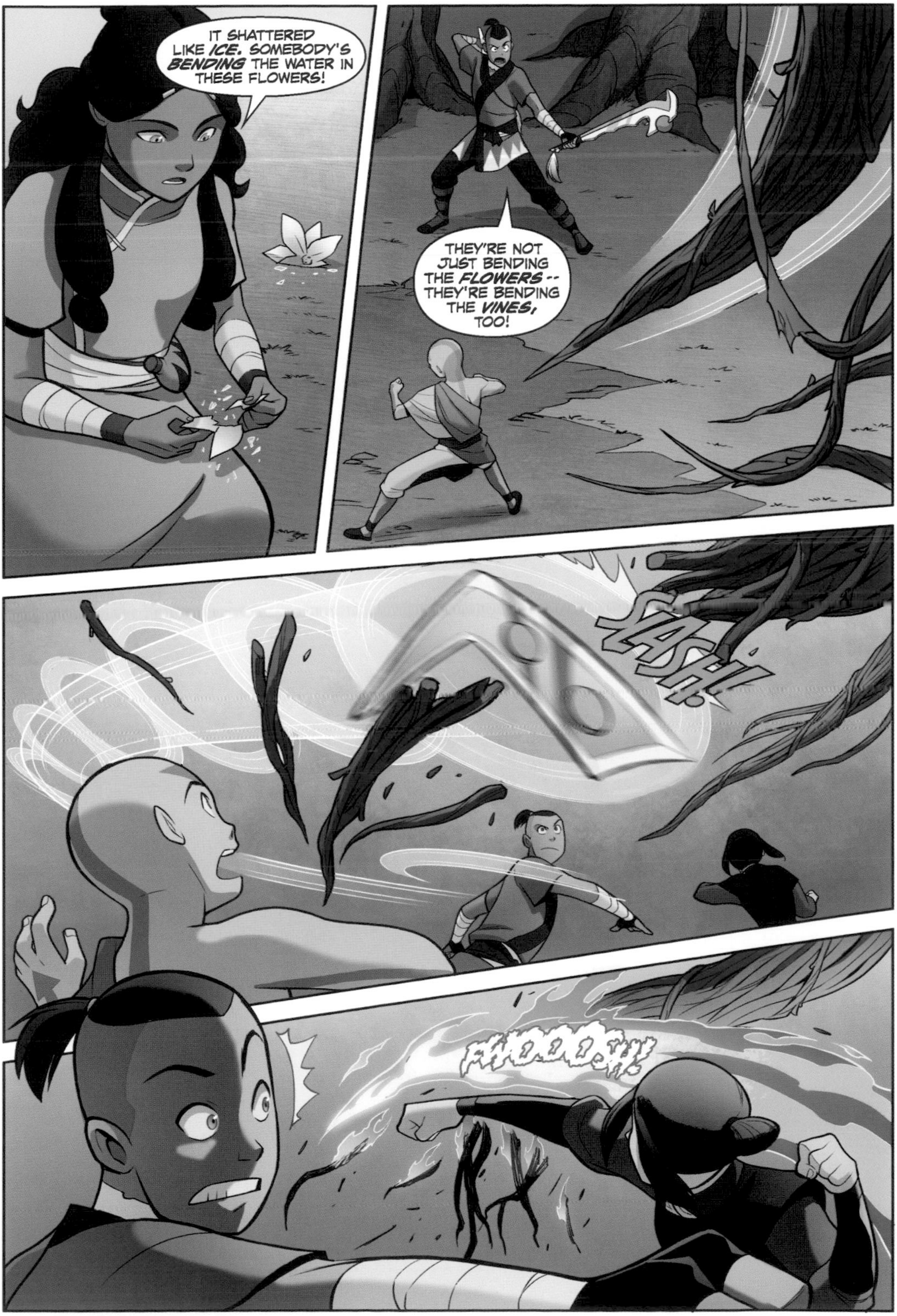
IT SHATTERED LIKE *ICE.* SOMEBODY'S *BENDING* THE WATER IN THESE FLOWERS!
THEY'RE NOT JUST BENDING THE *FLOWERS* -- THEY'RE BENDING THE *VINES,* TOO!
SASH!
FWOOOSH!

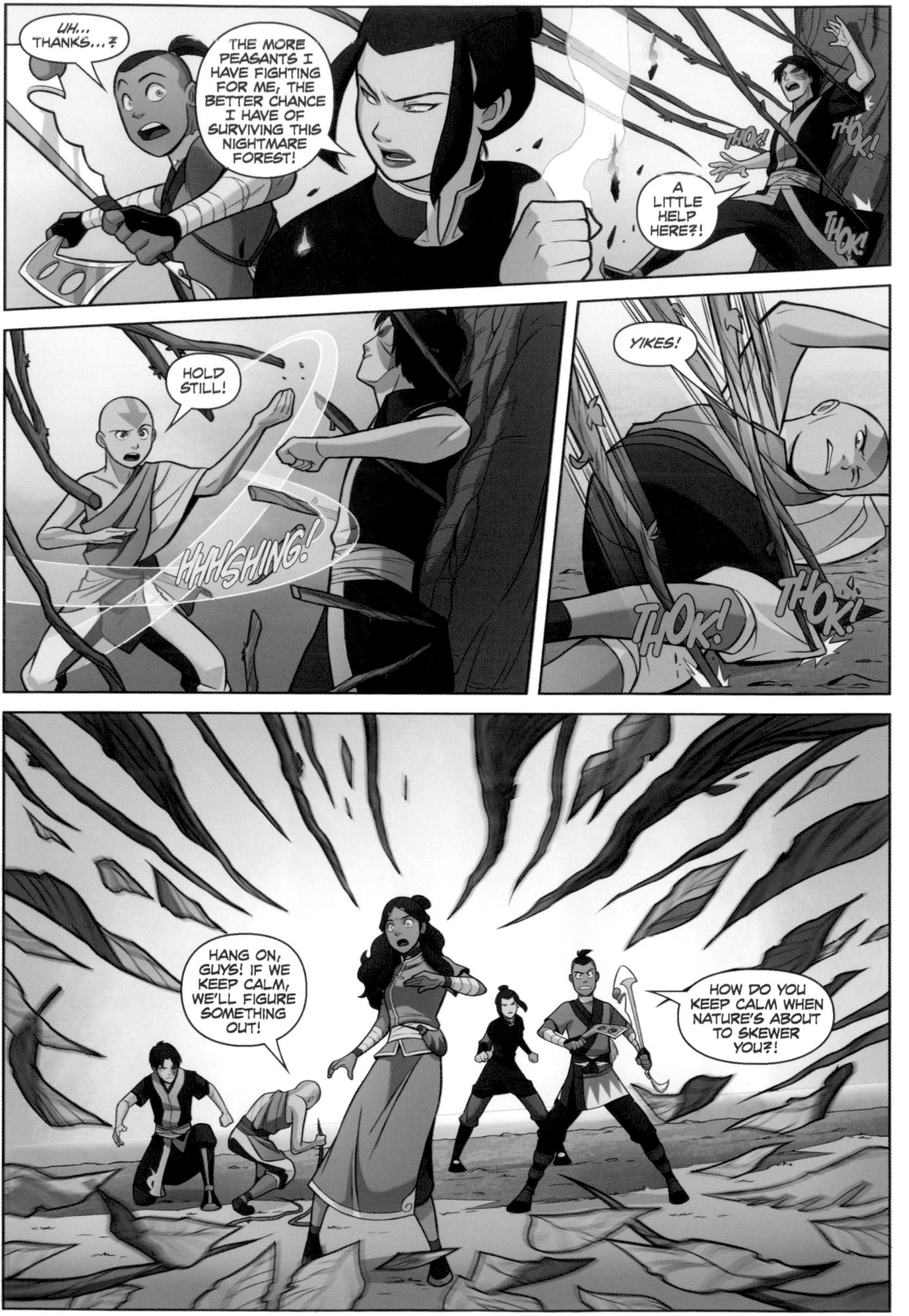
UH... THANKS...?
THE MORE PEASANTS I HAVE FIGHTING FOR ME, THE BETTER CHANCE I HAVE OF SURVIVING THIS NIGHTMARE FOREST!
THOK!
THOK!
A LITTLE HELP HERE?!
THOK!
HOLD STILL!
HHHSHING!
YIKES!
THOK!
THOK!
HANG ON, GUYS! IF WE KEEP CALM, WE'LL FIGURE SOMETHING OUT!
HOW DO YOU KEEP CALM WHEN NATURE'S ABOUT TO SKEWER YOU?!

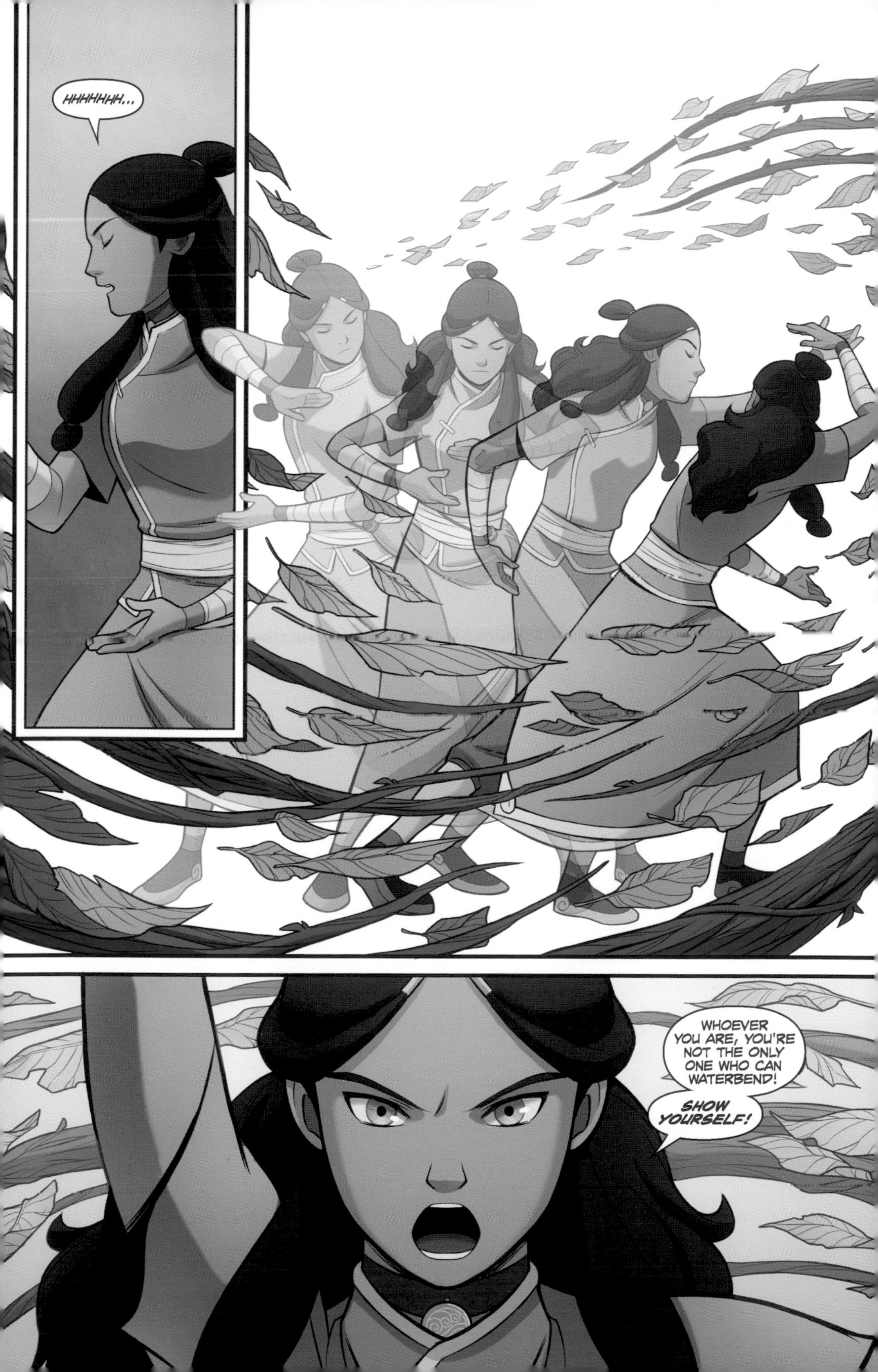
HHHHHHH...
WHOEVER YOU ARE, YOU'RE NOT THE ONLY ONE WHO CAN WATERBEND!
SHOW YOURSELF!

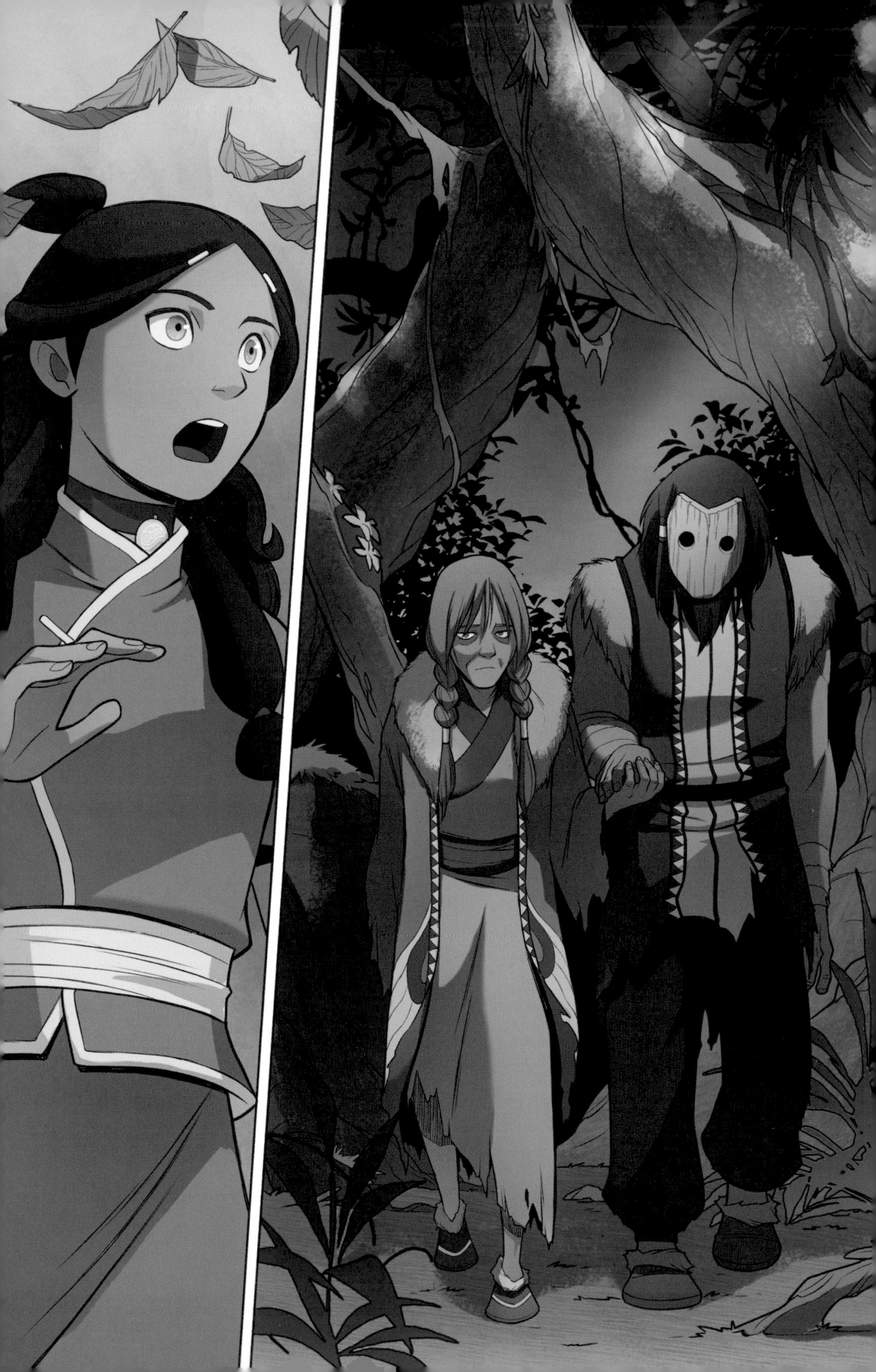

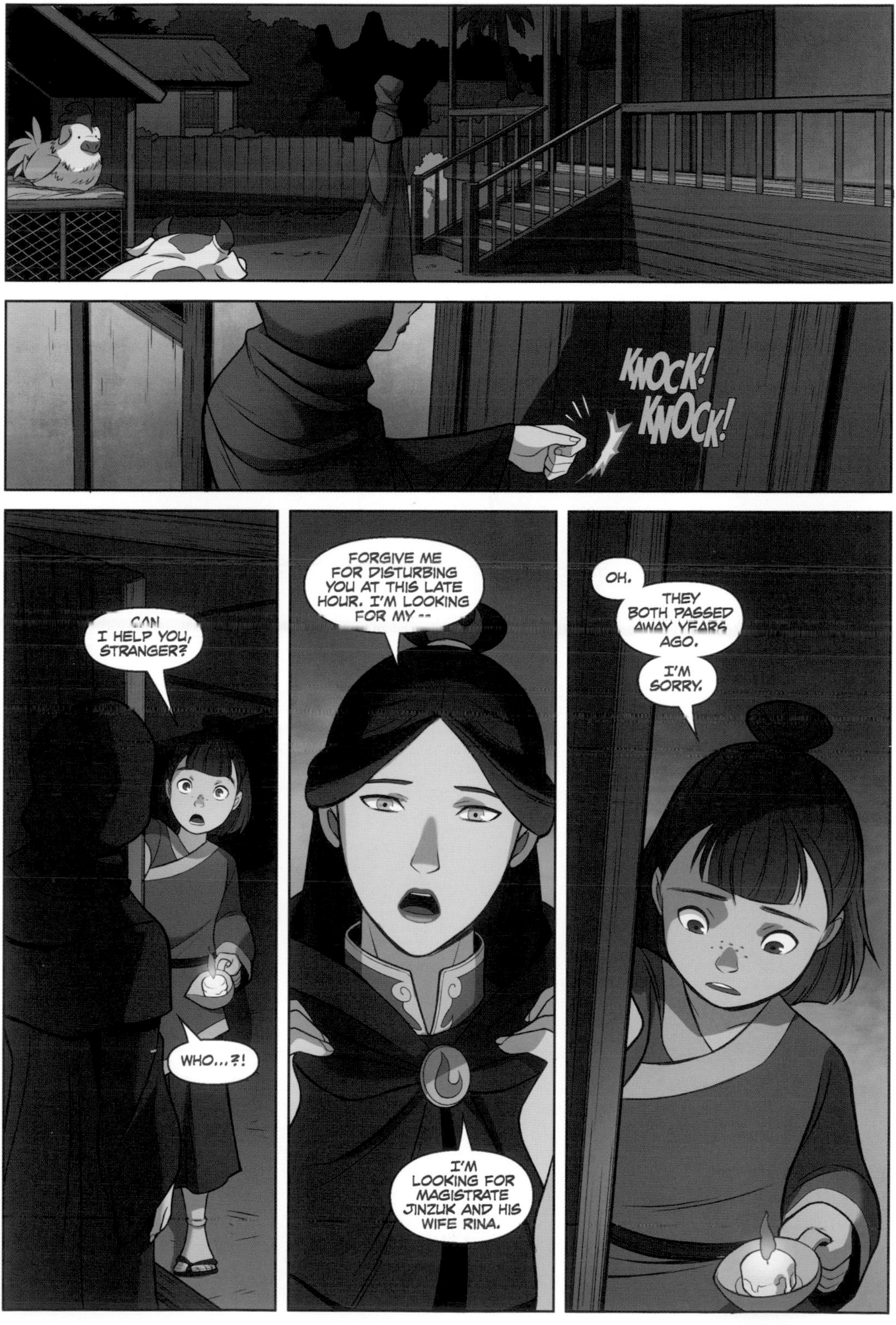
KNOCK! KNOCK!
CAN I HELP YOU, STRANGER?
WHO...?!
FORGIVE ME FOR DISTURBING YOU AT THIS LATE HOUR. I'M LOOKING FOR MY --
I'M LOOKING FOR MAGISTRATE JINZUK AND HIS WIFE RINA.
OH.
THEY BOTH PASSED AWAY YEARS AGO.
I'M SORRY.

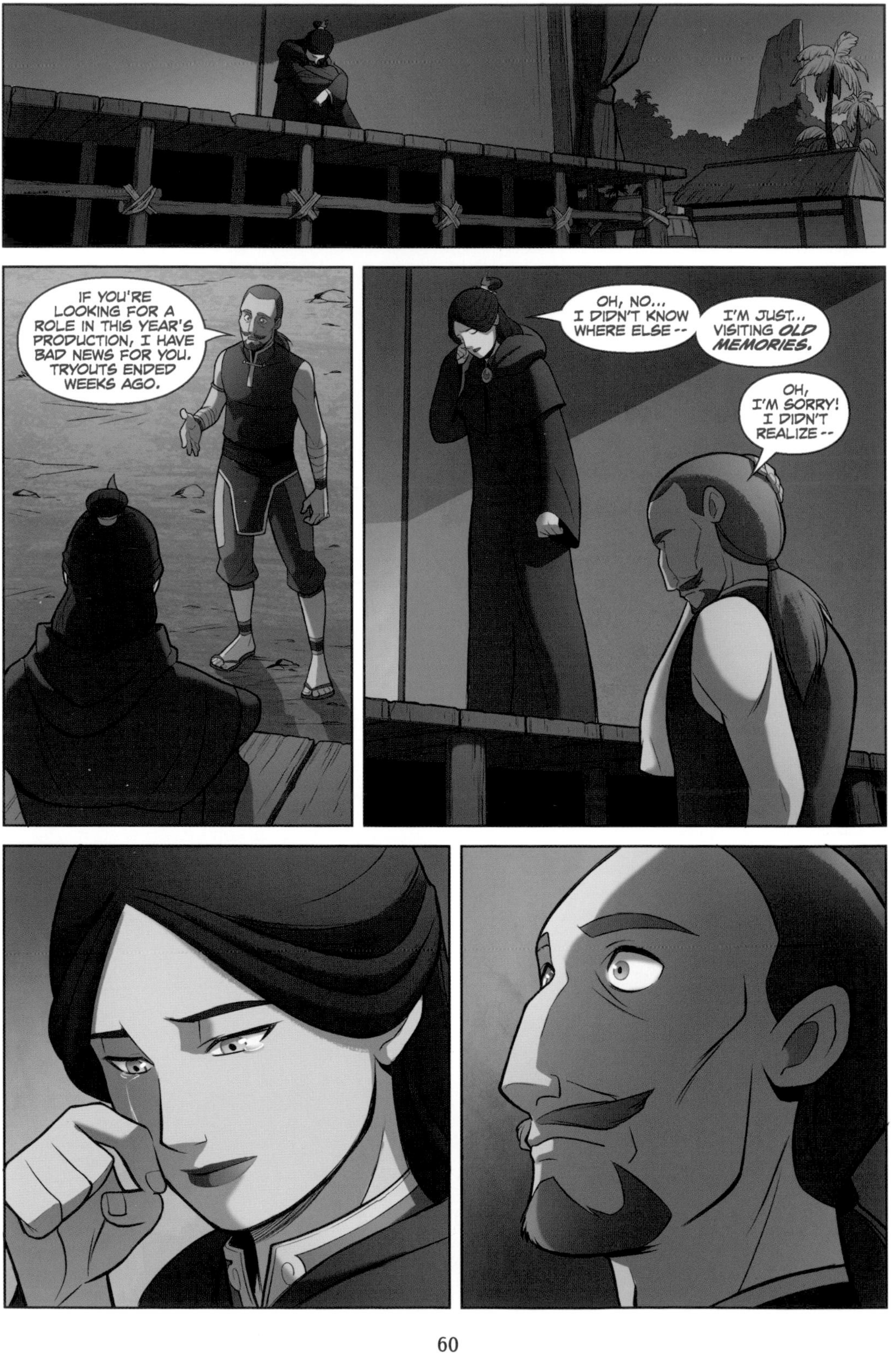
IF YOU'RE LOOKING FOR A ROLE IN THIS YEAR'S PRODUCTION, I HAVE BAD NEWS FOR YOU. TRYOUTS ENDED WEEKS AGO.
OH, NO... I DIDN'T KNOW WHERE ELSE --
I'M JUST... VISITING *OLD MEMORIES.*
OH, I'M SORRY! I DIDN'T REALIZE --

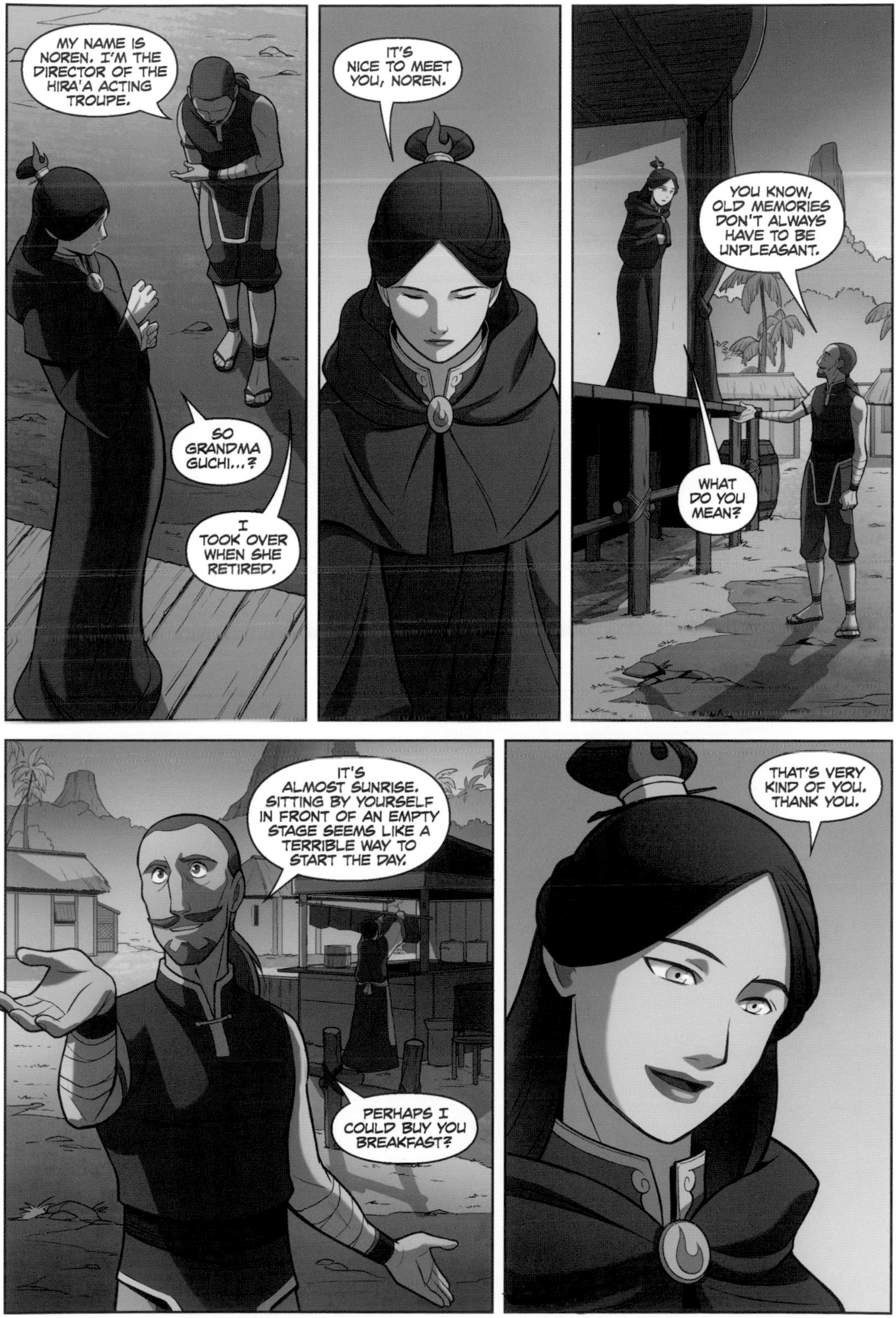
MY NAME IS NOREN. I'M THE DIRECTOR OF THE HIRA'A ACTING TROUPE.
SO GRANDMA GUCHI...?
I TOOK OVER WHEN SHE RETIRED.
IT'S NICE TO MEET YOU, NOREN.
YOU KNOW, OLD MEMORIES DON'T ALWAYS HAVE TO BE UNPLEASANT.
WHAT DO YOU MEAN?
IT'S ALMOST SUNRISE. SITTING BY YOURSELF IN FRONT OF AN EMPTY STAGE SEEMS LIKE A TERRIBLE WAY TO START THE DAY.
PERHAPS I COULD BUY YOU BREAKFAST?
THAT'S VERY KIND OF YOU. THANK YOU.

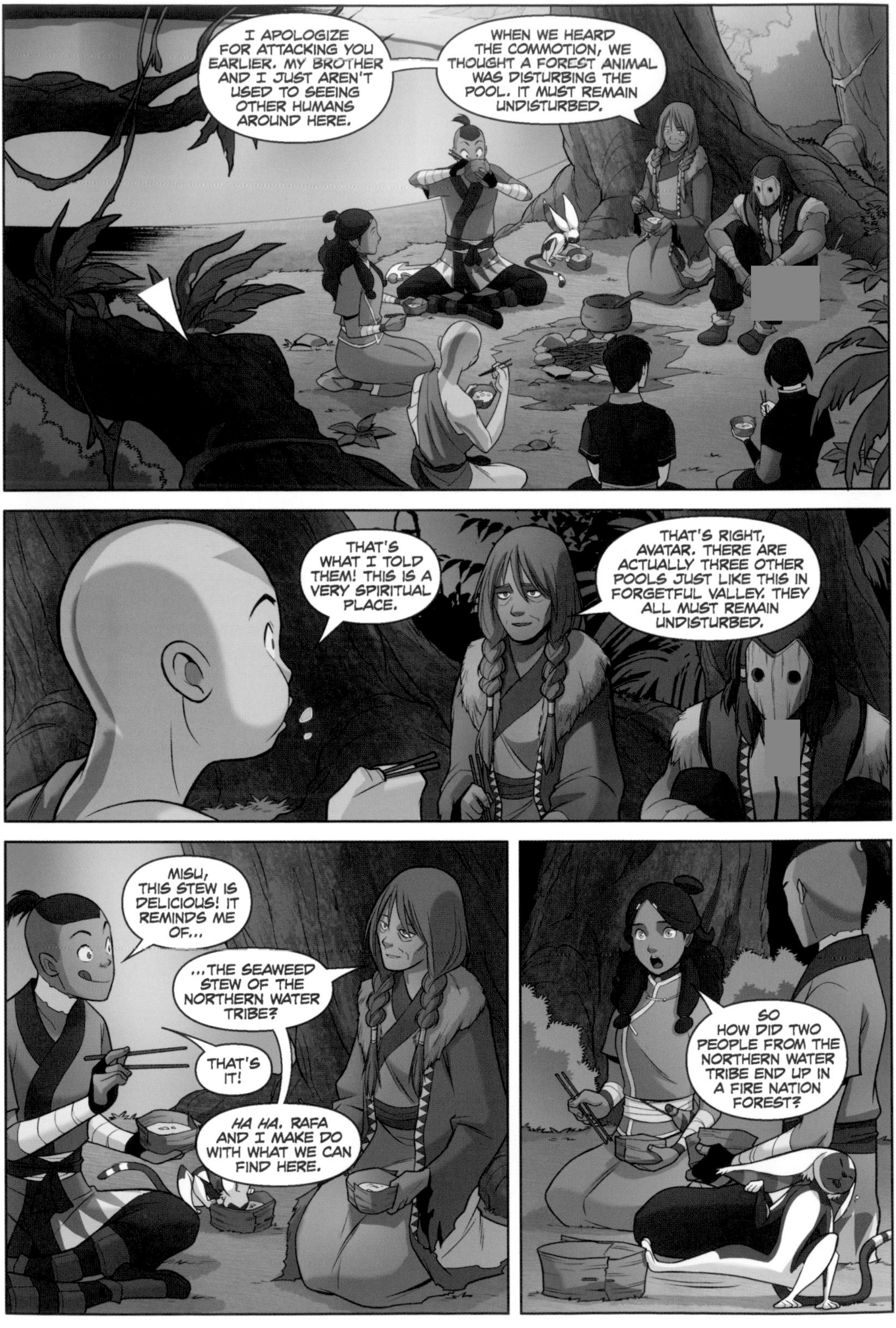
I APOLOGIZE FOR ATTACKING YOU EARLIER. MY BROTHER AND I JUST AREN'T USED TO SEEING OTHER HUMANS AROUND HERE.
WHEN WE HEARD THE COMMOTION, WE THOUGHT A FOREST ANIMAL WAS DISTURBING THE POOL. IT MUST REMAIN UNDISTURBED.
THAT'S WHAT I TOLD THEM! THIS IS A VERY SPIRITUAL PLACE.
THAT'S RIGHT, AVATAR. THERE ARE ACTUALLY THREE OTHER POOLS JUST LIKE THIS IN FORGETFUL VALLEY. THEY ALL MUST REMAIN UNDISTURBED.
MISU, THIS STEW IS DELICIOUS! IT REMINDS ME OF...
...THE SEAWEED STEW OF THE NORTHERN WATER TRIBE?
THAT'S IT!
HA HA. RAFA AND I MAKE DO WITH WHAT WE CAN FIND HERE.
SO HOW DID TWO PEOPLE FROM THE NORTHERN WATER TRIBE END UP IN A FIRE NATION FOREST?

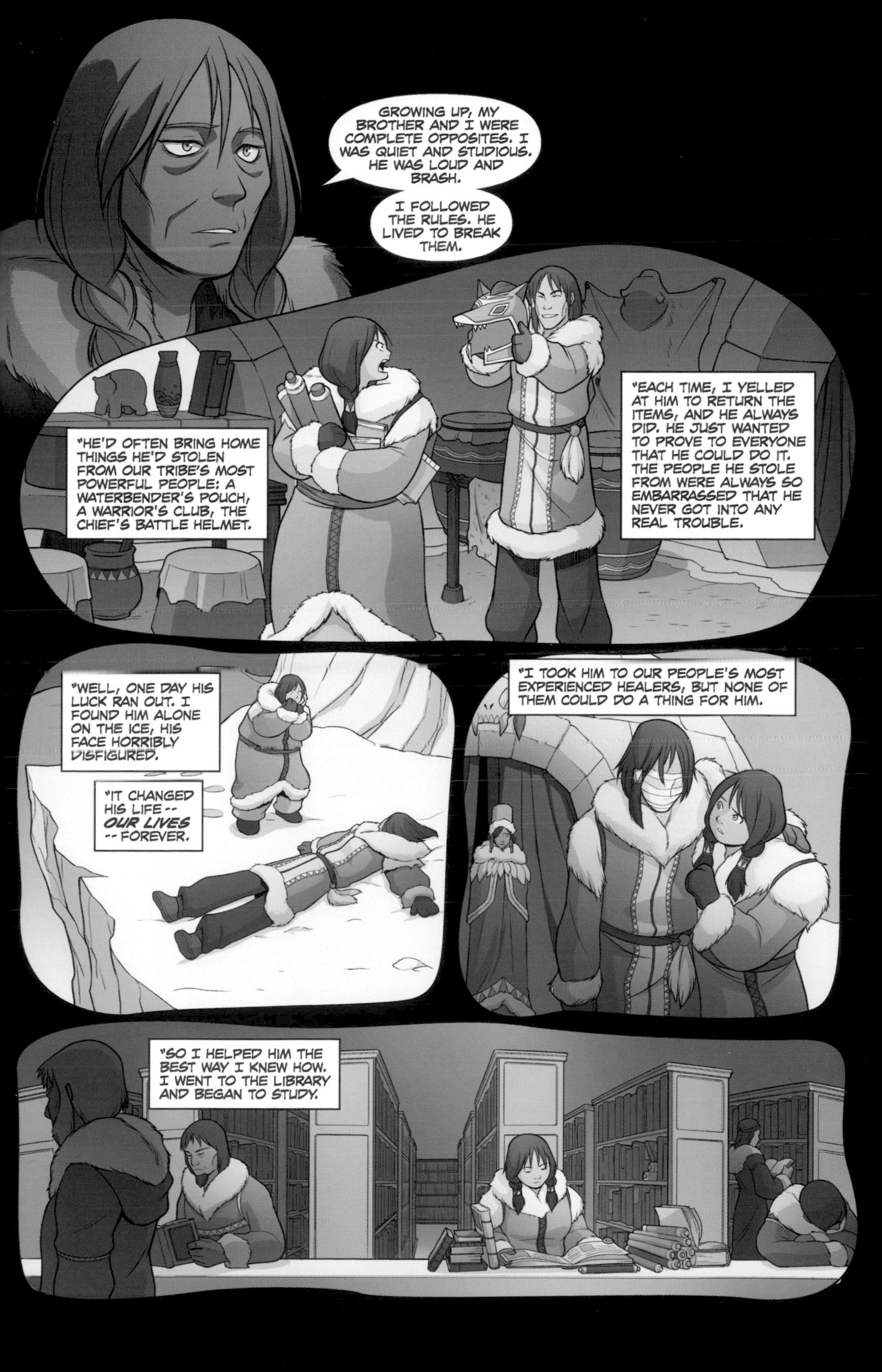
GROWING UP, MY BROTHER AND I WERE COMPLETE OPPOSITES. I WAS QUIET AND STUDIOUS. HE WAS LOUD AND BRASH.
I FOLLOWED THE RULES. HE LIVED TO BREAK THEM.
"HE'D OFTEN BRING HOME THINGS HE'D STOLEN FROM OUR TRIBE'S MOST POWERFUL PEOPLE: A WATERBENDER'S POUCH, A WARRIOR'S CLUB, THE CHIEF'S BATTLE HELMET.
"EACH TIME, I YELLED AT HIM TO RETURN THE ITEMS, AND HE ALWAYS DID. HE JUST WANTED TO PROVE TO EVERYONE THAT HE COULD DO IT. THE PEOPLE HE STOLE FROM WERE ALWAYS SO EMBARRASSED THAT HE NEVER GOT INTO ANY REAL TROUBLE.
"WELL, ONE DAY HIS LUCK RAN OUT. I FOUND HIM ALONE ON THE ICE, HIS FACE HORRIBLY DISFIGURED.
"IT CHANGED HIS LIFE -- *OUR LIVES* -- FOREVER.
"I TOOK HIM TO OUR PEOPLE'S MOST EXPERIENCED HEALERS, BUT NONE OF THEM COULD DO A THING FOR HIM.
"SO I HELPED HIM THE BEST WAY I KNEW HOW. I WENT TO THE LIBRARY AND BEGAN TO STUDY.

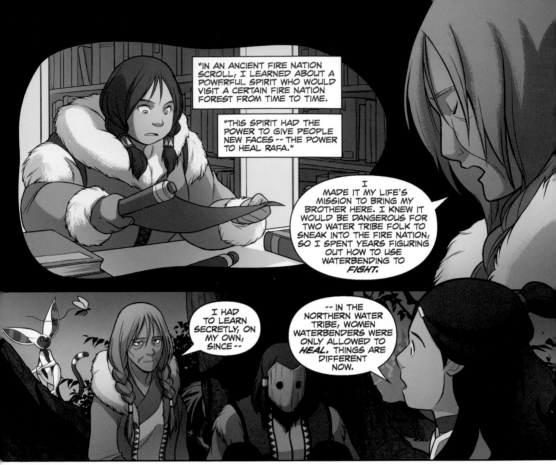

"IN AN ANCIENT FIRE NATION SCROLL, I LEARNED ABOUT A POWERFUL SPIRIT WHO WOULD VISIT A CERTAIN FIRE NATION FOREST FROM TIME TO TIME.

"THIS SPIRIT HAD THE POWER TO GIVE PEOPLE NEW FACES -- THE POWER TO HEAL RAFA."

I MADE IT MY LIFE'S MISSION TO BRING MY BROTHER HERE. I KNEW IT WOULD BE DANGEROUS FOR TWO WATER TRIBE FOLK TO SNEAK INTO THE FIRE NATION, SO I SPENT YEARS FIGURING OUT HOW TO USE WATERBENDING TO *FIGHT*.

I HAD TO LEARN SECRETLY, ON MY OWN, SINCE --

-- IN THE NORTHERN WATER TRIBE, WOMEN WATERBENDERS WERE ONLY ALLOWED TO *HEAL*. THINGS ARE DIFFERENT NOW.

AFTER MANY FAILED ATTEMPTS, WE FINALLY MADE IT TO FORGETFUL VALLEY. WE'VE LIVED HERE EVER SINCE, HOPING TO ENCOUNTER THE SPIRIT.

HOW COME RAFA HASN'T EATEN ANYTHING?

64

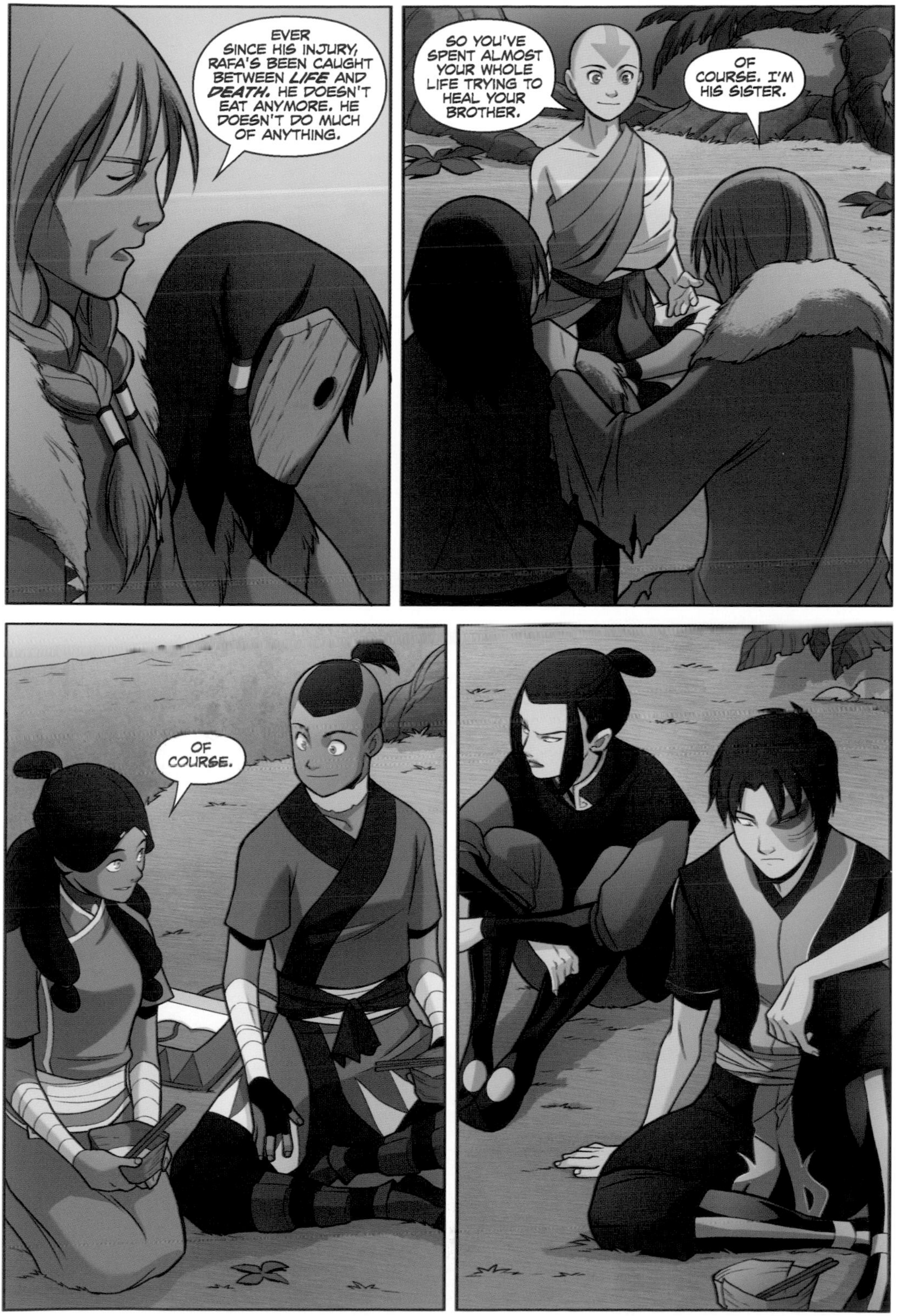
EVER SINCE HIS INJURY, RAFA'S BEEN CAUGHT BETWEEN *LIFE* AND *DEATH.* HE DOESN'T EAT ANYMORE. HE DOESN'T DO MUCH OF ANYTHING.
SO YOU'VE SPENT ALMOST YOUR WHOLE LIFE TRYING TO HEAL YOUR BROTHER.
OF COURSE. I'M HIS SISTER.
OF COURSE.

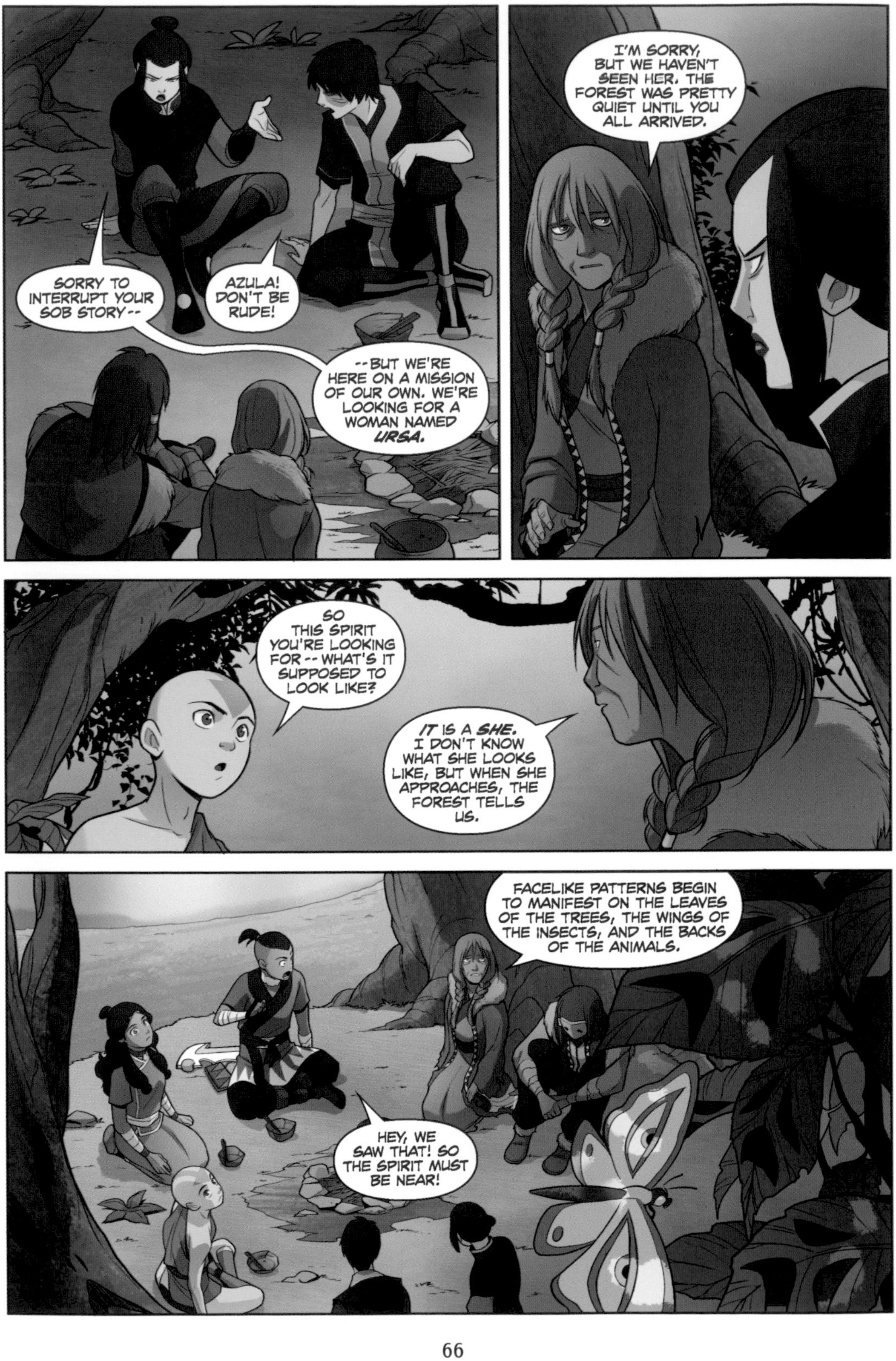
SORRY TO INTERRUPT YOUR SOB STORY--
AZULA! DON'T BE RUDE!
--BUT WE'RE HERE ON A MISSION OF OUR OWN. WE'RE LOOKING FOR A WOMAN NAMED *URSA.*
I'M SORRY, BUT WE HAVEN'T SEEN HER. THE FOREST WAS PRETTY QUIET UNTIL YOU ALL ARRIVED.
SO THIS SPIRIT YOU'RE LOOKING FOR--WHAT'S IT SUPPOSED TO LOOK LIKE?
IT IS A *SHE.* I DON'T KNOW WHAT SHE LOOKS LIKE, BUT WHEN SHE APPROACHES, THE FOREST TELLS US.
FACELIKE PATTERNS BEGIN TO MANIFEST ON THE LEAVES OF THE TREES, THE WINGS OF THE INSECTS, AND THE BACKS OF THE ANIMALS.
HEY, WE SAW THAT! SO THE SPIRIT MUST BE NEAR!

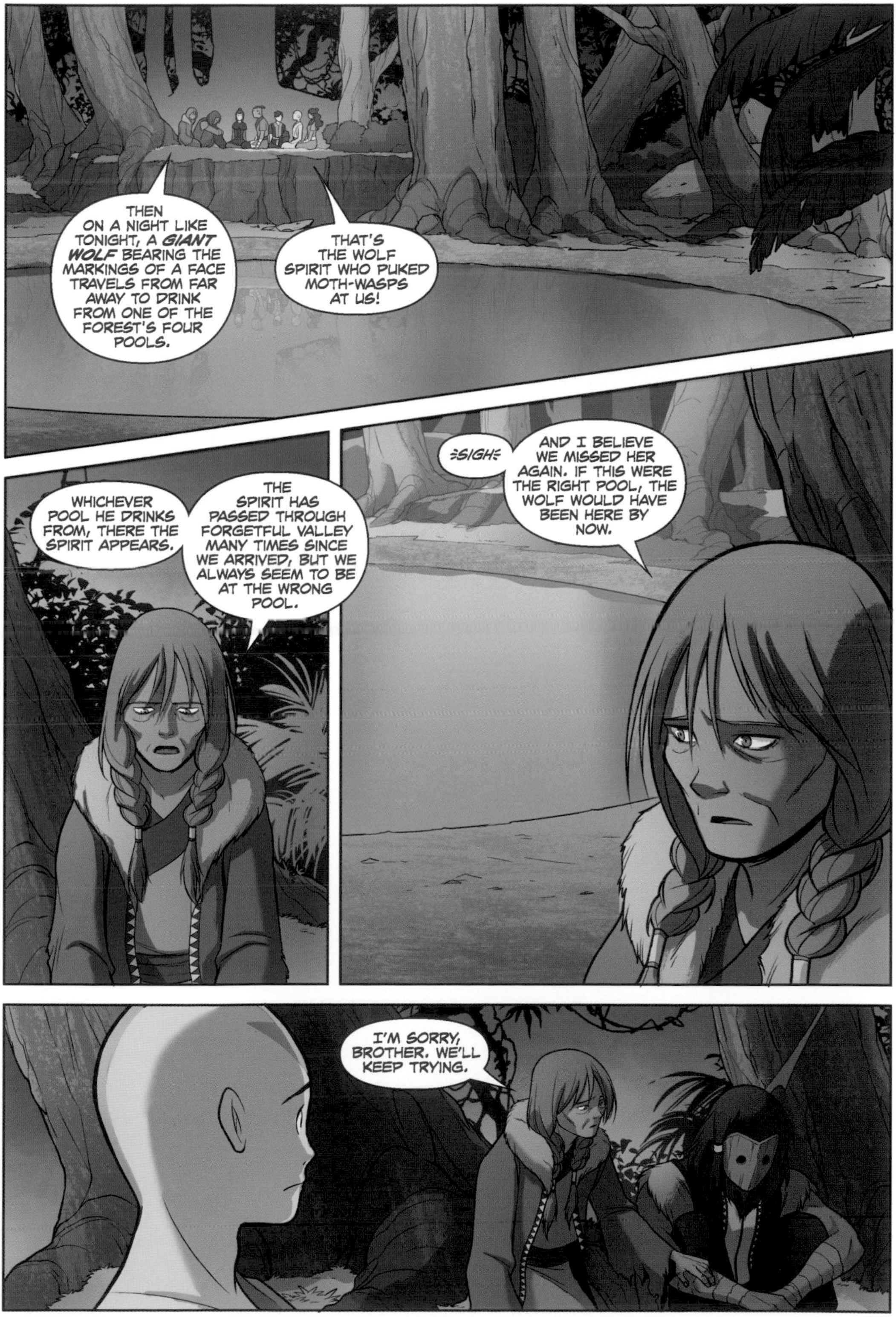
THEN ON A NIGHT LIKE TONIGHT, A GIANT WOLF BEARING THE MARKINGS OF A FACE TRAVELS FROM FAR AWAY TO DRINK FROM ONE OF THE FOREST'S FOUR POOLS.
THAT'S THE WOLF SPIRIT WHO PUKED MOTH-WASPS AT US!
WHICHEVER POOL HE DRINKS FROM, THERE THE SPIRIT APPEARS.
THE SPIRIT HAS PASSED THROUGH FORGETFUL VALLEY MANY TIMES SINCE WE ARRIVED, BUT WE ALWAYS SEEM TO BE AT THE WRONG POOL.
SIGH
AND I BELIEVE WE MISSED HER AGAIN. IF THIS WERE THE RIGHT POOL, THE WOLF WOULD HAVE BEEN HERE BY NOW.
I'M SORRY, BROTHER. WE'LL KEEP TRYING.

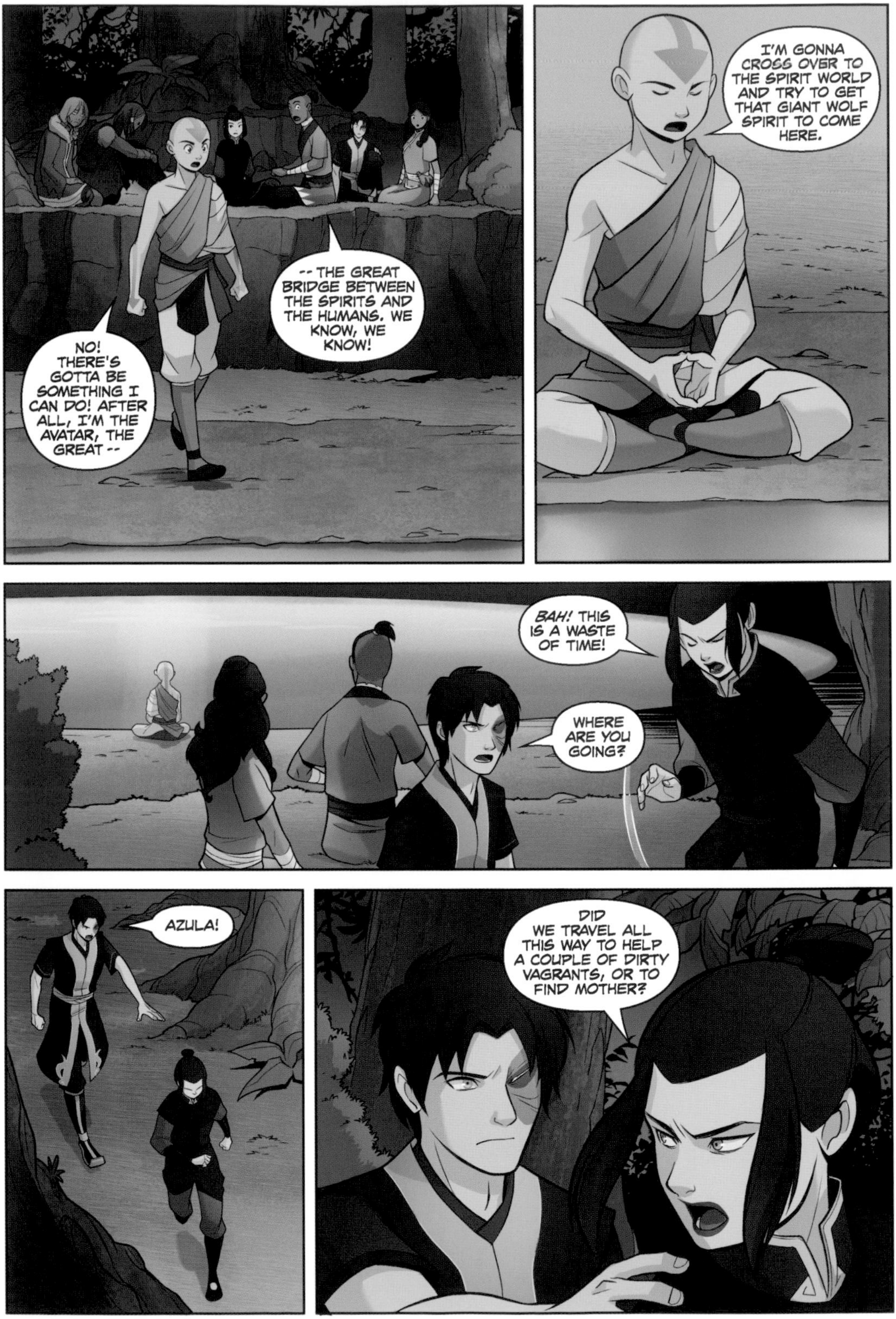
NO! THERE'S GOTTA BE SOMETHING I CAN DO! AFTER ALL, I'M THE AVATAR, THE GREAT --
-- THE GREAT BRIDGE BETWEEN THE SPIRITS AND THE HUMANS. WE KNOW, WE KNOW!
I'M GONNA CROSS OVER TO THE SPIRIT WORLD AND TRY TO GET THAT GIANT WOLF SPIRIT TO COME HERE.
BAH! THIS IS A WASTE OF TIME!
WHERE ARE YOU GOING?
AZULA!
DID WE TRAVEL ALL THIS WAY TO HELP A COUPLE OF DIRTY VAGRANTS, OR TO FIND MOTHER?

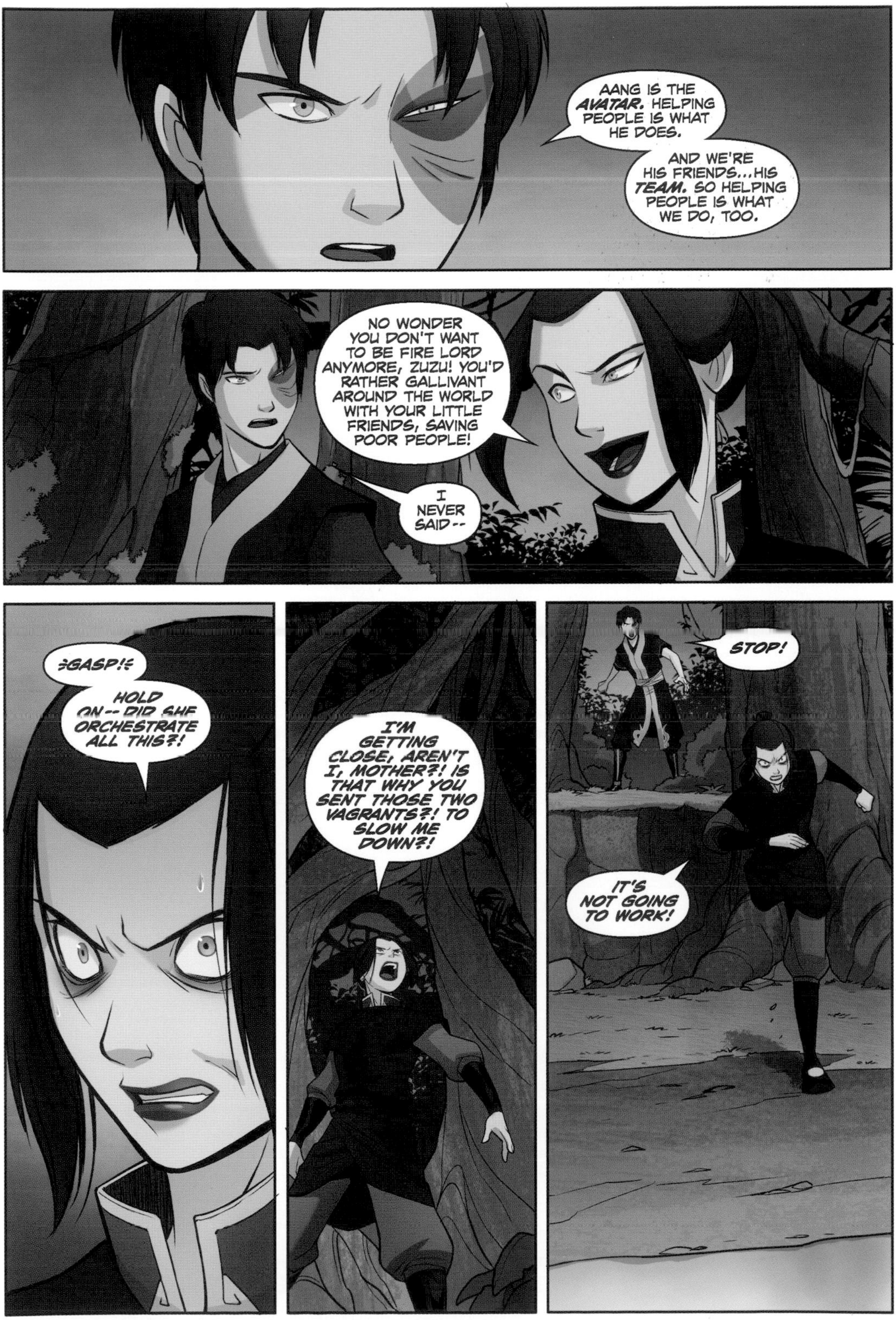
AANG IS THE *AVATAR.* HELPING PEOPLE IS WHAT HE DOES.
AND WE'RE HIS FRIENDS...HIS *TEAM.* SO HELPING PEOPLE IS WHAT WE DO, TOO.
NO WONDER YOU DON'T WANT TO BE FIRE LORD ANYMORE, ZUZU! YOU'D RATHER GALLIVANT AROUND THE WORLD WITH YOUR LITTLE FRIENDS, SAVING POOR PEOPLE!
I NEVER SAID--
GASP!
HOLD ON-- DID SHE ORCHESTRATE ALL THIS?!
I'M GETTING CLOSE, AREN'T I, MOTHER?! IS THAT WHY YOU SENT THOSE TWO VAGRANTS?! TO SLOW ME DOWN?!
STOP!
IT'S NOT GOING TO WORK!

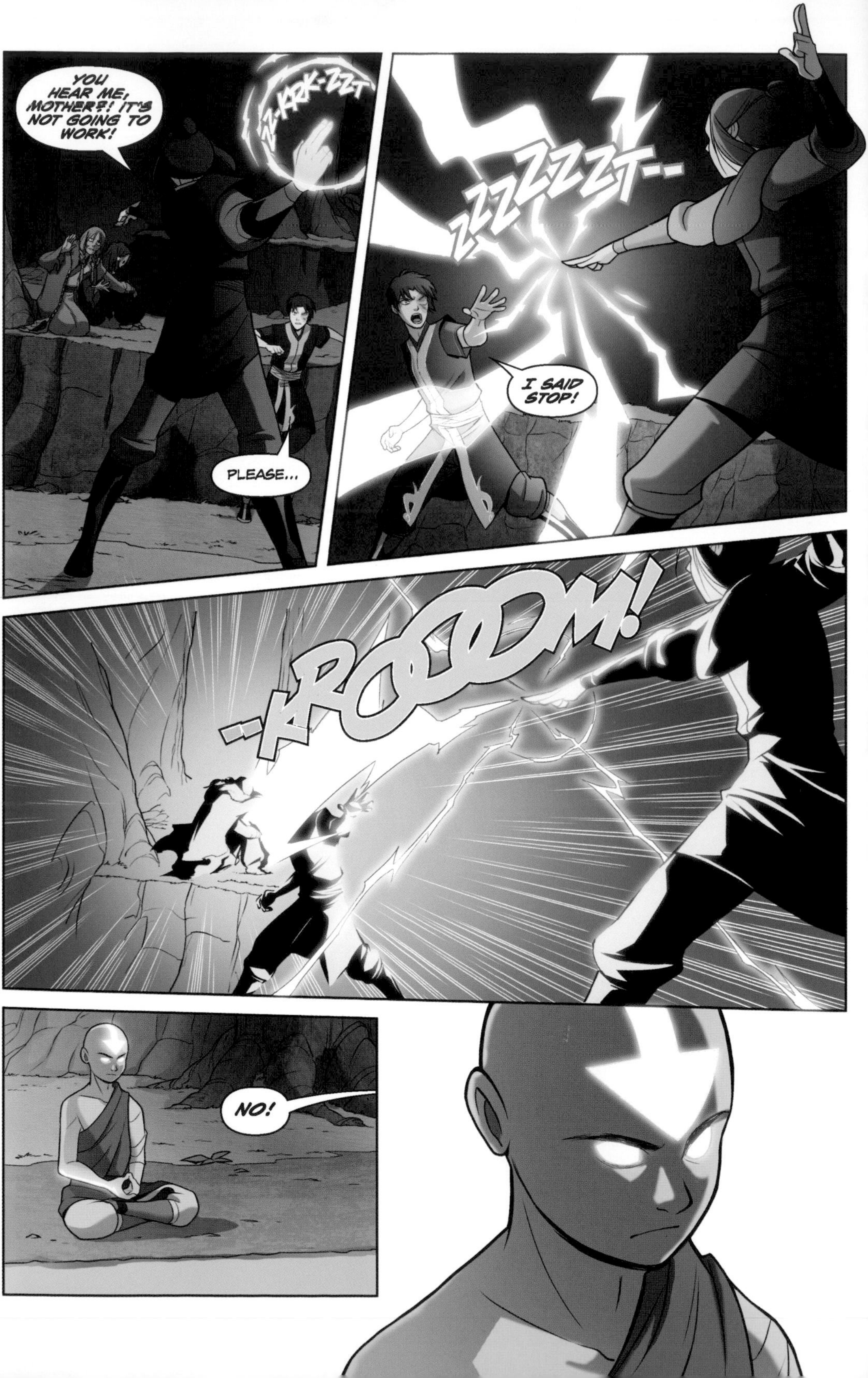
YOU HEAR ME, MOTHER?! IT'S NOT GOING TO WORK!
ZZ-KRK-ZZ-T
PLEASE...
ZZZZZZT--
I SAID STOP!
--KROOOOM!
NO!

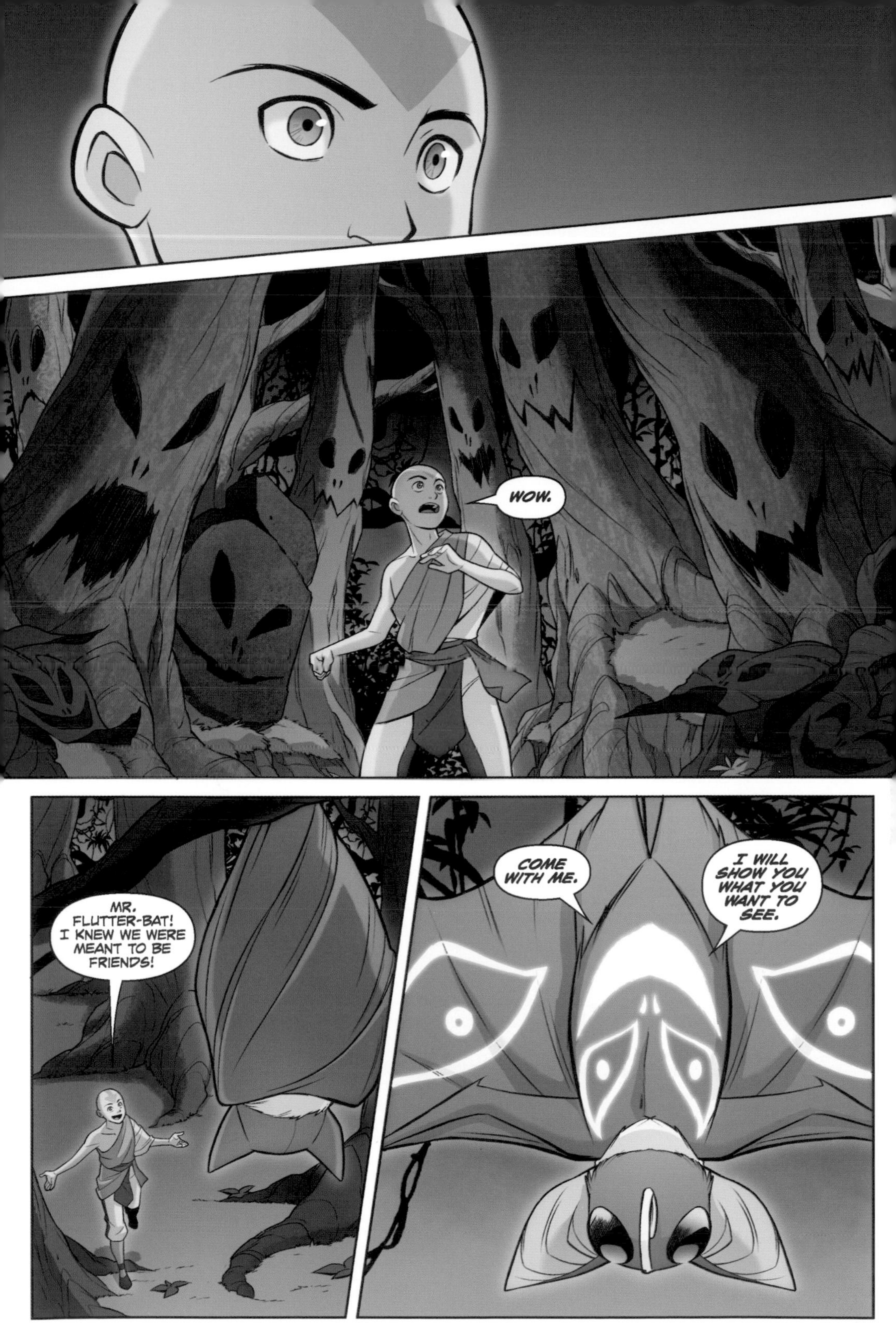
WOW.
MR. FLUTTER-BAT! I KNEW WE WERE MEANT TO BE FRIENDS!
COME WITH ME.
I WILL SHOW YOU WHAT YOU WANT TO SEE.

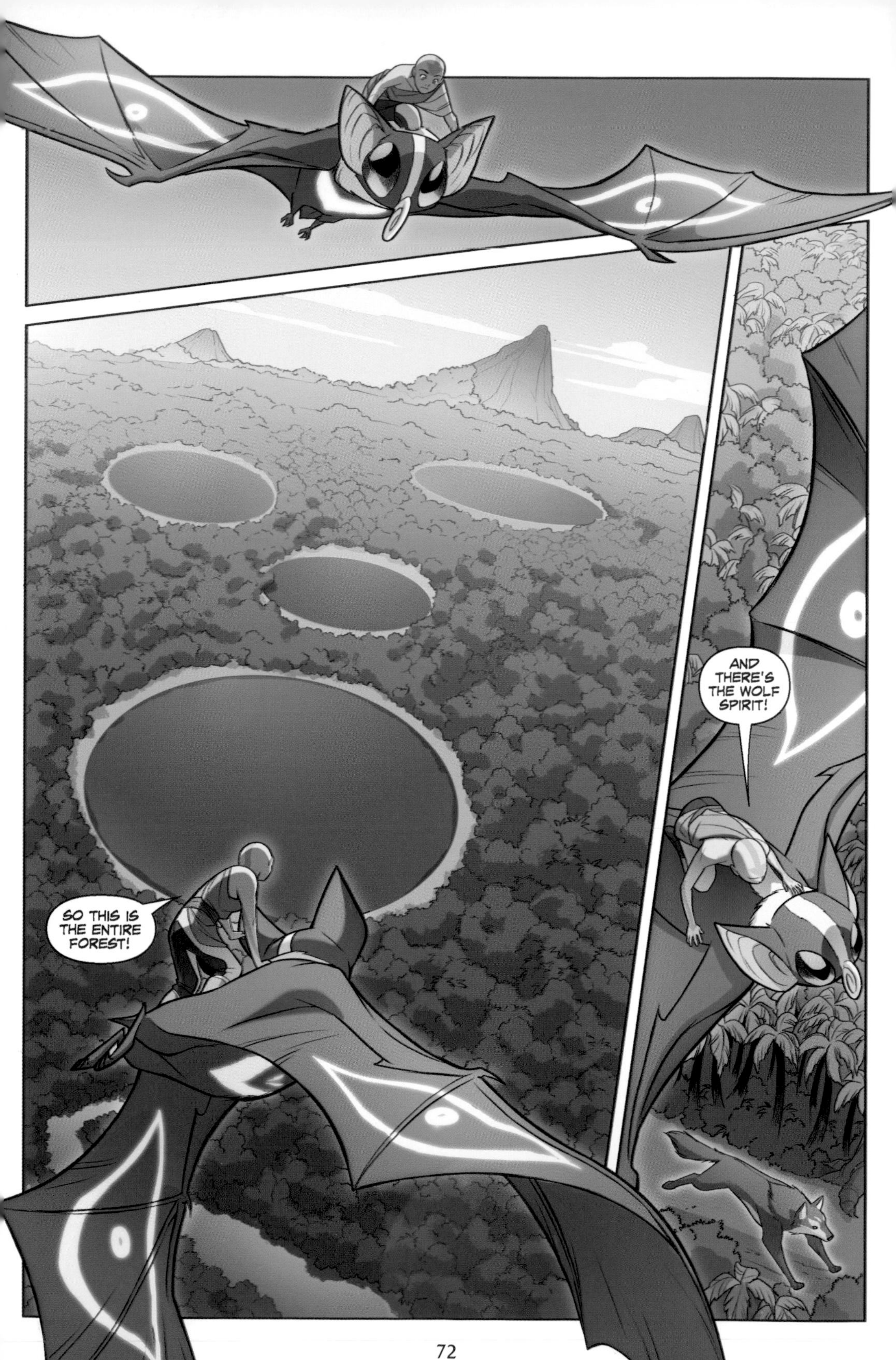
SO THIS IS THE ENTIRE FOREST!
AND THERE'S THE WOLF SPIRIT!

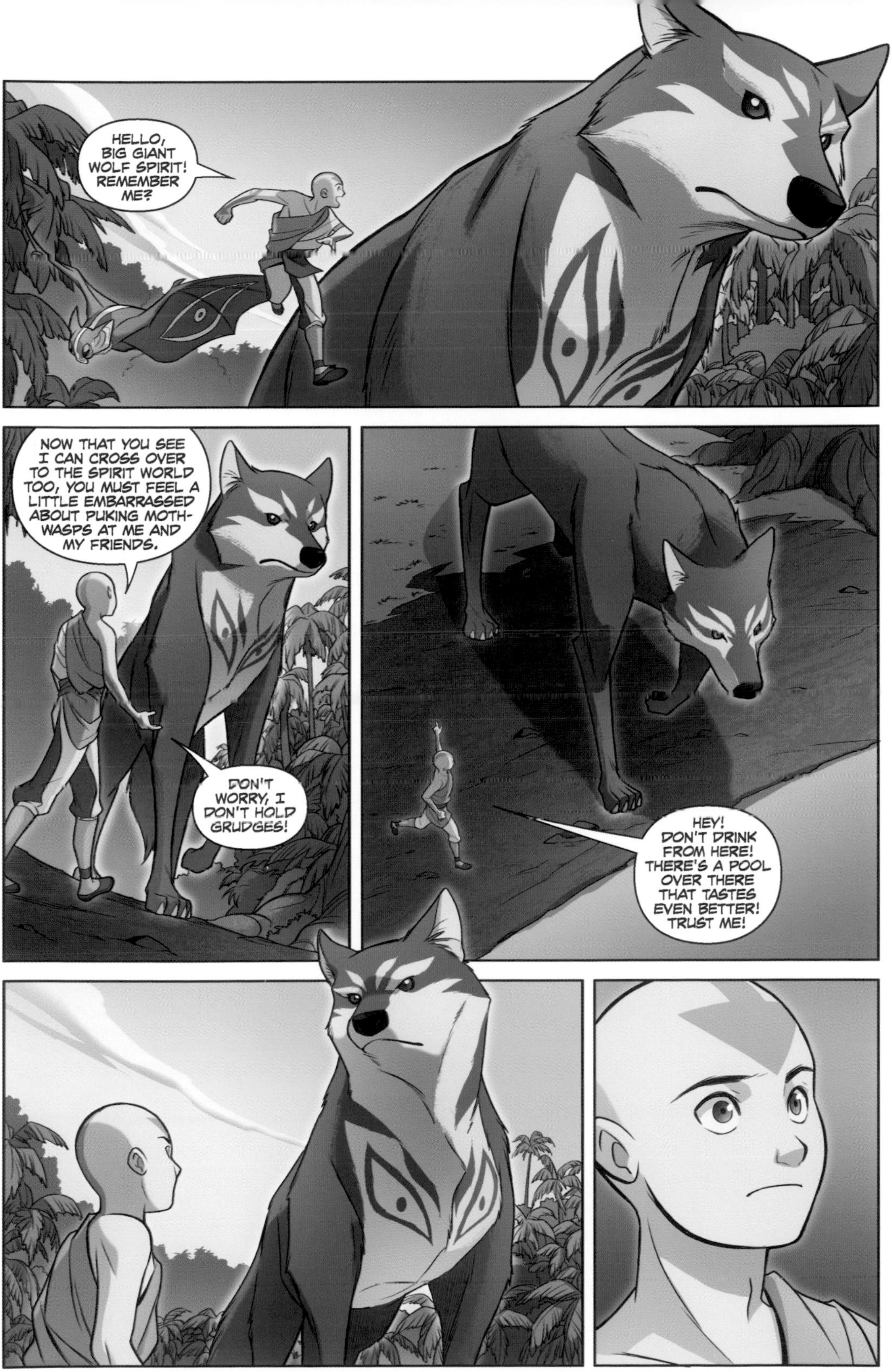
HELLO, BIG GIANT WOLF SPIRIT! REMEMBER ME?
NOW THAT YOU SEE I CAN CROSS OVER TO THE SPIRIT WORLD TOO, YOU MUST FEEL A LITTLE EMBARRASSED ABOUT PUKING MOTH-WASPS AT ME AND MY FRIENDS.
DON'T WORRY, I DON'T HOLD GRUDGES!
HEY! DON'T DRINK FROM HERE! THERE'S A POOL OVER THERE THAT TASTES EVEN BETTER! TRUST ME!

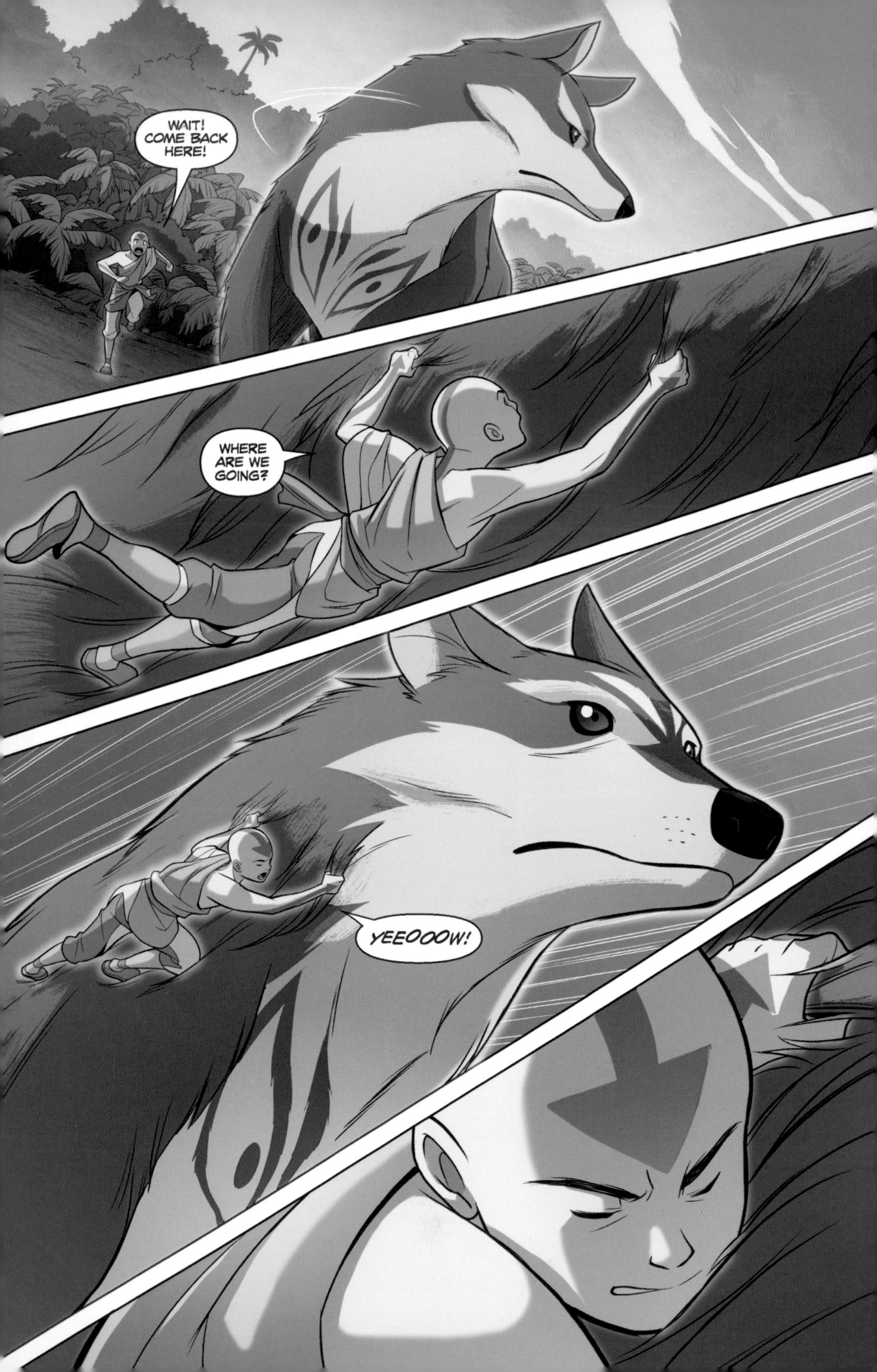
WAIT! COME BACK HERE!
WHERE ARE WE GOING?
YEEOOOW!

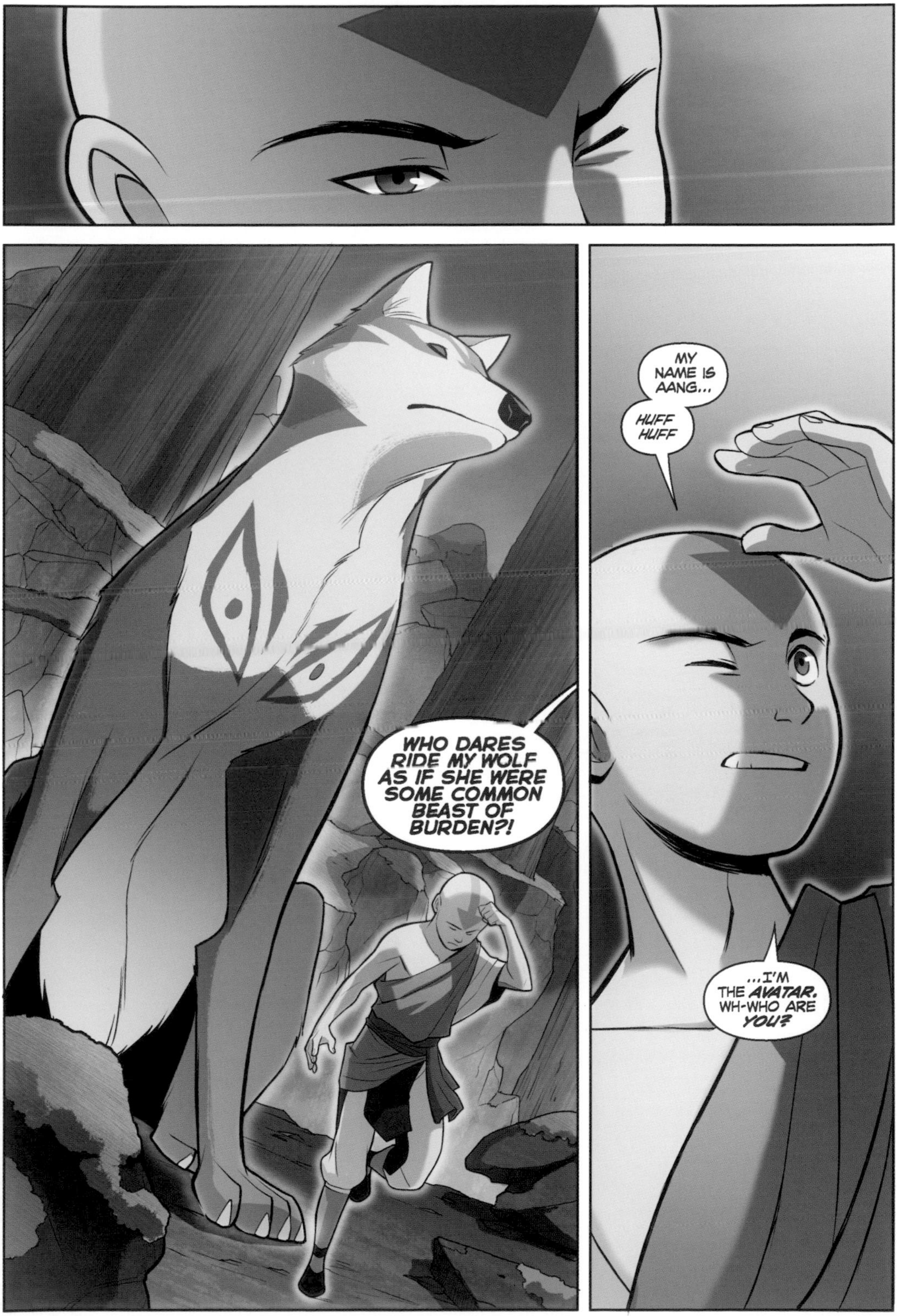
WHO DARES RIDE MY WOLF AS IF SHE WERE SOME COMMON BEAST OF BURDEN?!
MY NAME IS AANG...
HUFF HUFF
...I'M THE AVATAR. WH-WHO ARE YOU?

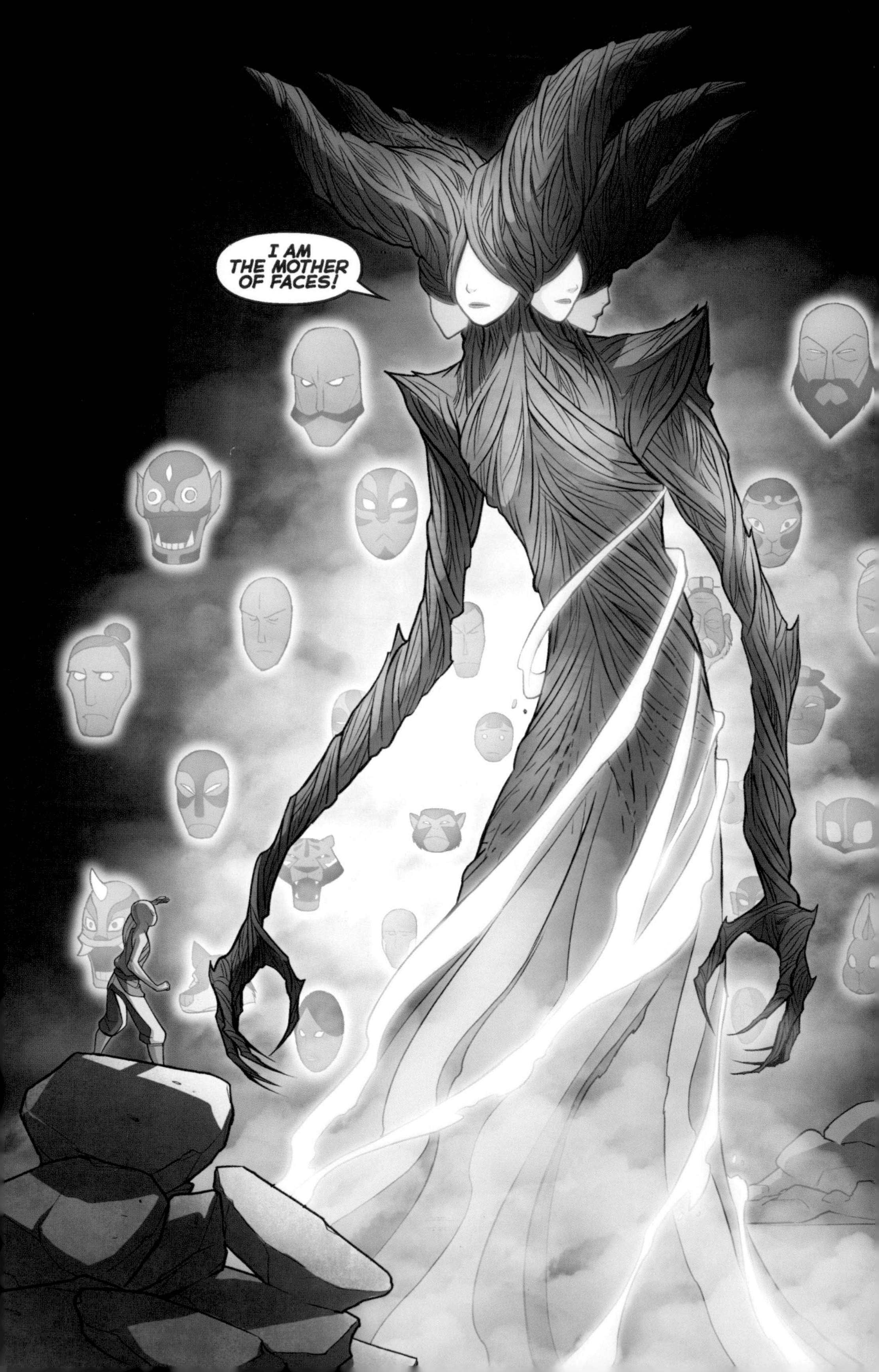
I AM THE MOTHER OF FACES!

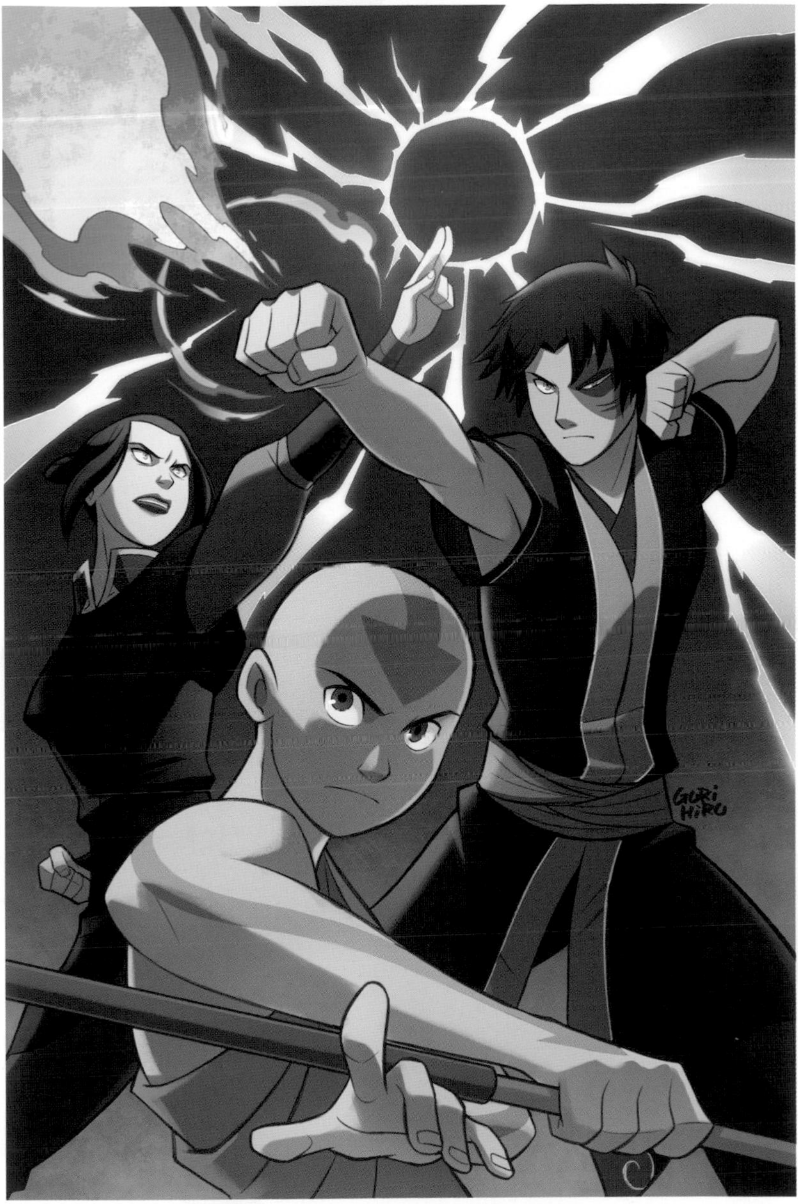
GURI HIRU

COMING IN OCTOBER

The fate of Zuko's mother revealed in . . .

THE SEARCH • PART THREE

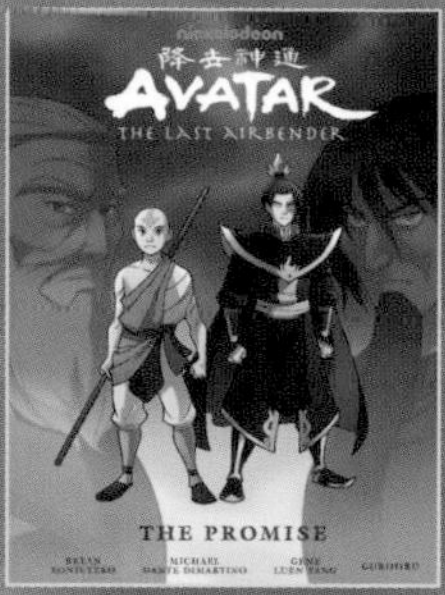
nickelodeon
AVATAR
THE LAST AIRBENDER
THE PROMISE

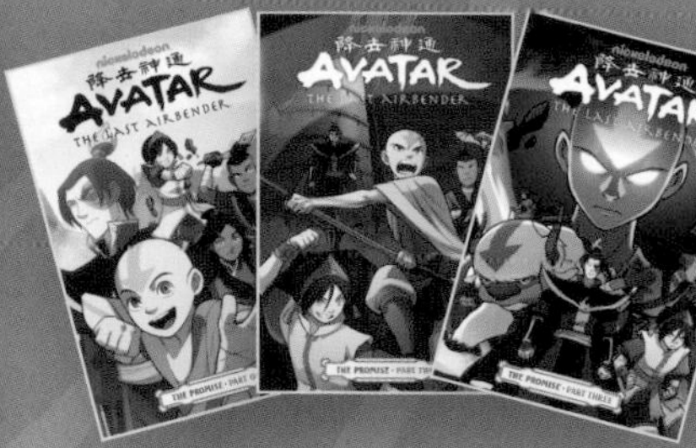
AVATAR
THE LAST AIRBENDER

Avatar: The Last Airbender—The Promise Library Edition
978-1-61655-074-5 $39.99

Avatar: The Last Airbender—The Promise Part 1
978-1-59582-811-8 $10.99

Avatar: The Last Airbender—The Promise Part 2
978-1-59582-875-0 $10.99

Avatar: The Last Airbender—The Promise Part 3
978-1-59582-941-2 $10.99

Avatar: The Last Airbender—The Search Library Edition
978-1-61655-226-8 $39.99

Avatar: The Last Airbender—The Search Part 1
978-1-61655-054-7 $10.99

Avatar: The Last Airbender—The Search Part 2
978-1-61655-190-2 $10.99

Avatar: The Last Airbender—The Search Part 3
978-1-61655-184-1 $10.99

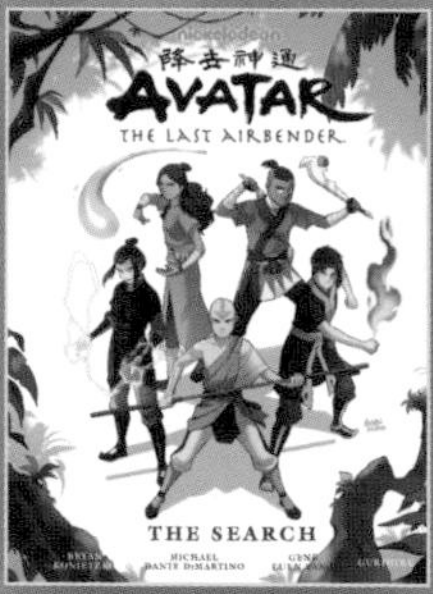
nickelodeon
AVATAR
THE LAST AIRBENDER
THE SEARCH

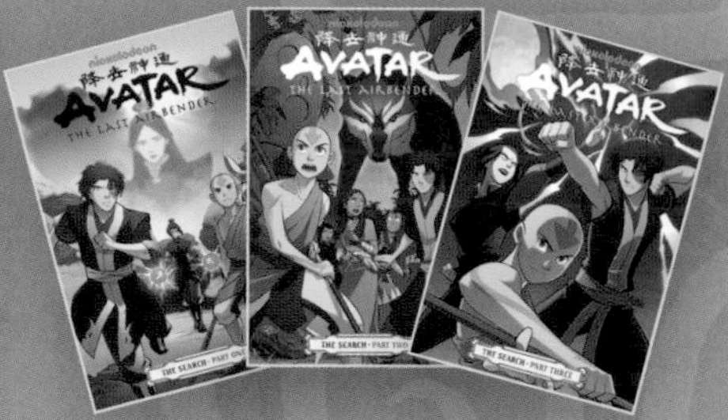
AVATAR
THE LAST AIRBENDER

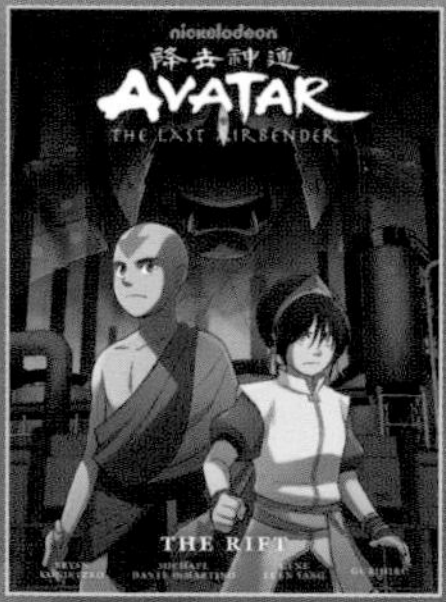
nickelodeon
AVATAR
THE LAST AIRBENDER
THE RIFT

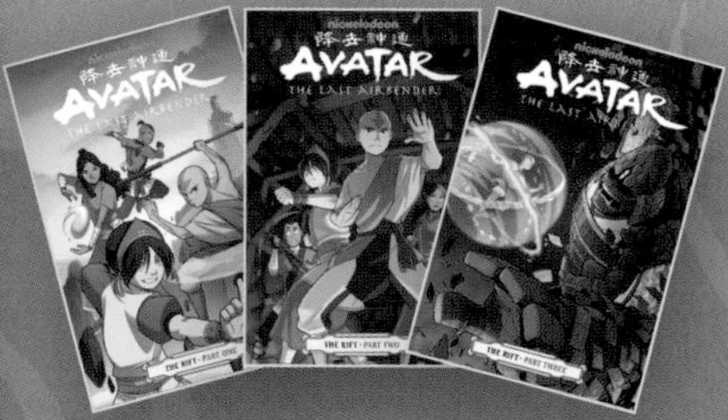
AVATAR
THE LAST AIRBENDER

Avatar: The Last Airbender—The Rift Library Edition
978-1-61655-550-4 $39.99

Avatar: The Last Airbender—The Rift Part 1
978-1-61655-295-4 $10.99

Avatar: The Last Airbender—The Rift Part 2
978-1-61655-296-1 $10.99

Avatar: The Last Airbender—The Rift Part 3
978-1-61655-297-8 $10.99

Avatar: The Last Airbender—Smoke and Shadow Library Edition
978-1-50670-013-7 $39.99

Avatar: The Last Airbender—Smoke and Shadow Part 1
978-1-61655-761-4 $10.99

Avatar: The Last Airbender—Smoke and Shadow Part 2
978-1-61655-790-4 $10.99

Avatar: The Last Airbender—Smoke and Shadow Part 3
978-1-61655-838-3 $10.99

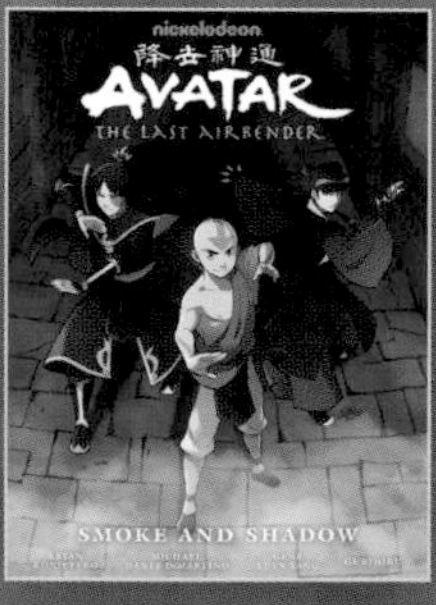
nickelodeon
AVATAR
THE LAST AIRBENDER
SMOKE AND SHADOW

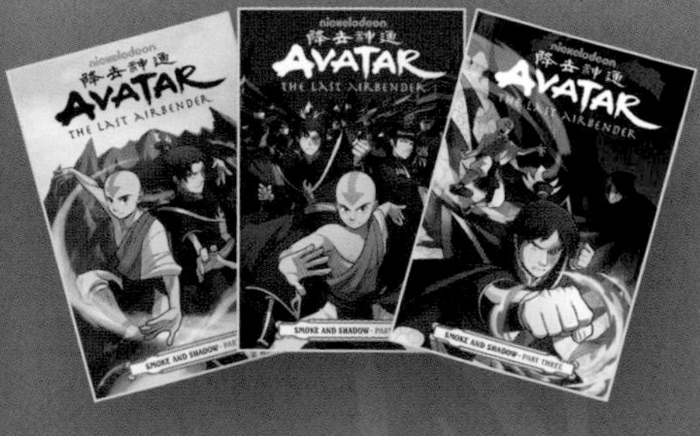
AVATAR
THE LAST AIRBENDER